Gems From My Father's River

by

Brian R. Weeks

Gems From My Father's River

Copyright © 2018 – Brian R. Weeks

Published by **Vision Publishing**

Ramona, California

ISBN 978-1-7294-2209-0

FOR INFORMATION ON ORDERING PLEASE CONTACT:

Vision Publishing

1-800-9VISION

www.visionpublishingservices.com

PRINTED IN THE UNITED STATES OF AMERICA

RECOMMENDATIONS

The amazing book, *Gems From My Father's River,* was written by our beloved friend, Pastor Brian Weeks. In this book he shares his unbelievable life and so many experiences - the good, the bad, and the ugly. Reading it will encourage you to see the best in yourself and in others.

If you're struggling with reputation, if your life has been hell on earth, if you have a hard time being content, or even have a tendency to limit God, as you start digging through the pages of this book you will find beautiful gems and answers for that which you've searched for, perhaps for a very long time. No doubt it can be the kickoff of an exciting new life!

Jose Gabriel Cabral
Senior Pastor – Conquerors for Christ Church
President & Founder - Care for Children International, Inc.

Throughout this book, you will find well documented stories; they are lessons learned in the crucible of life. Pastor Brian's transparency begs us to examine our own souls to see how his personal experiences, personal feelings, and personal shortcomings may mirror our own. How might the wisdom he learned help us in our own personal journey?

Within the pages of this book, you will discover gems of knowledge and nuggets of gold mined from the river of life. The wisdom he learned along the way is here for the taking. After reading through the first portion of this book, I sent Pastor Brian a message. I told him, Brian, your book is like the balm of Gilead, salve for the soul.

I have come to look forward with anticipation to reading each of Pastor Brian Weeks' books. The newest, *Gems From My Father's River*, is no exception; it is yet another phenomenal book.

Dr. Kathy J. Smith
VIU Communications Coordinator
Director of Vision Publishing

In a time, they're calling the Fatherless Generation, I find Pastor Brian's book so timely and appropriate. How correct were the Apostle Paul's words that we have many teachers but few fathers.

I love this book because not only does it anchor us in the Kingdom through the reality of His Word, but it comes from the Life of a practitioner who is able to put into words his experiences. These in turn take us further than knowledge into a place of transition where the Word in us is made Spirit, enabling us to be truly empowered. Pastor Brian allows us to be unafraid of our humanity, knowing that God's Grace that is lavished on us through Christ not only takes our sins and sickness, but is more than enough to see us through our dark moments. Those moments in turn make us strong.

Thank you, Pastor Brian for the years of being on the coal face of life as well as in the river of your God picking up the Gems. You are a true Father of the Faith. We need a lot more of your breed to raise up Sons who truly desire to leave a legacy of true Sonship on the earth. I know whoever reads this book is going to be encouraged to run for God knowing there is nothing that will separate them from their Father's love.

In fact, the reader will be willing to run to make Sons and Daughters, proud of who they are. *Gems From My Father's River* truly makes Great Reading.

Be Blessed!

Fergus McIntyre
Global Mission, Australia

ACKNOWLEGEMENTS

After I left college in 1970 I was faced with a choice. I could go home and investigate whether God was real or go west and attempt a career as a writer. Thankfully I chose to go home.

Turns out the second desire was simply put on hold.

Yes, even as time passed, the desire to write was deep within me and didn't disappear. Until recently though, I was too busy and furthermore, honestly, had nothing to say. Then about five or six years ago when thoughts began coming to my mind, I started writing them down, which led to Thoughts of the Day, a devotional which I posted (and still do) daily. Eventually I compiled them into my first book Musings. Then came Divine Encounters. Both were published in 2017.

Yes, I waited 47 years to write! And now I have finished my third book.

I address all this by way of praising God for his faithfulness. To have kept the dream of writing alive has literally kept me alive. I thank God and acknowledge that I am being truly empowered to write. For the past six months I tried to write this book but couldn't - there was no anointing. Then one day I heard, "Go write," and within a very short time book three was done. Thank you, Holy Spirit!

I want to acknowledge all the people in my life who I've met or walked beside since the day I committed my life to Christ. I have learned so much, and without them this book would not have been written. Of them I ask for forgiveness for any wrong actions or attitudes that surfaced within our relationship or in the midst of our even brief encounters.

To my wife Donna and son and daughter Josh and Crystal, thank you for who you are and for the love and encouragement you have given me.

Thank you again to Anne Kaminski for her continued encouragement and hours of editing – her calls for clarification and further development of parts of the text as well as all the grammatical errors she has fixed. Truth be told, without her I don't see how this book or my first two would've ever been published. I could have paid an editor (but not really, as I couldn't have afforded it), but likely they would not have invested their heart and mind by asking the same questions or requiring the same clarification. I'll say it again, thank you Anne...

TABLE OF CONTENTS

Introduction

Revelation 22:1-2 The Passion Translation

"Then the angel showed me the river of the water of life, flowing with water clear as crystal, continuously pouring out from the throne of God and of the Lamb."

I have used the term "gems" to express how precious and valuable is the nature of each of the concepts and principles in this book. The idea of using the river from Revelation 22 is that this river flows from the very throne of God, carrying along His presence.

For many years the Holy Spirit would give me insight into various scriptures and how they could specifically impact my daily life. Unfortunately, I didn't take the time to write them down because I was always looking for the next revelation. I liken it to a gold miner panning for gold. When he finds a small nugget, he sees it and doesn't assign it any value because he's looking for a larger one. The funny thing is, if I had valued each nugget no matter its size and then one by one put them together, I would have seen that the larger nugget I was waiting for was already in my possession!

All along God was giving me these awesome gems, many of which I no longer recall. So what I am doing now is collecting each nugget and recording them so as to assign honor to what He has graciously shown me.

I also feel that some of the things I have discovered and learned could perhaps impart some wisdom and revelation into other's lives and am delighted to think that some of them would be a benefit and blessing to you.

My desire is that the "gems" in this book give you, the reader, insight and revelation which will impact your life for the better…

My deepest love and affection to you all,

pb

Your Identity

Perhaps the biggest thing I've learned over these 48 years is about my true identity. If in this entire book I'm writing you glean one thing, it would be to know your true identity.

For so many years my identity was as a pastor. I failed to see, however, that being a pastor was simply my function. Along with this false identity came a very real but subtle form of pride.

I have to laugh when I read "he put me into the ministry," because for years I took credit for something I really had nothing to do with. First Timothy 1:12 says, "And I thank Christ Jesus our Lord who has enabled me, because He counted me faithful, putting me into the ministry." (NKJV)

Unfortunately for years and years I didn't understand that my true identity is as God's son. And you yourself are God's son or daughter.

I have been adopted. Romans 8:15 (NKJV): "For you did not receive the spirit of bondage again to fear, but you received the Spirit of adoption by whom we cry out, 'Abba, Father.' " Oh my, I AM GOD'S SON. Knowing that I had been adopted eliminated my need to be accepted. For years I was prisoner to the desire to be accepted, until I understood Ephesians 1:6 (NKJV) that He "made us accepted in the Beloved."

I am no longer a prisoner to performance. I no longer have to represent a ministry or a theology. I am called to be a reflection of my Father. John 14:9 (NKJV): "He who has seen Me has seen the Father." No greater purpose could I ever have but to somehow reflect my FATHER...

Having a false identity means always having to perform or put out a certain image. I don't have to do either of these things. I don't have to act (hypocrisy); I just have to be me. I have one desire and that is what Jesus said in John 8:29 (NKJV): "for I always do those things that please Him."

My true identity has eliminated my need and compulsion to live a life of striving. We were not created to strive. We were created to rest. Man was created on the sixth day, his first day being the sabbath. We were created to rest and to literally walk with him as Adam did in rest and in presence. In fact, the meaning of the word Eden (garden) means 'presence' in the Hebrew.

We are sons and daughters representing our father's Kingdom as his personal ambassadors. Second Corinthians 5:20 says, "We are ambassadors for Christ."

Every day when you wake up, look in the mirror and declare, "I am God's son," or "I am God's daughter."

No Wood, No Fire

People often wonder why the fire went out in their relationship with the Lord or even with their wife or husband. The answer can lie in the response to the questions, "Did I feed the fire? Did I put any wood on it?"

Proverbs 26:20 (NKJV) says, "Where there is no wood, the fire goes out." It goes on to say, (NET) "where there is no gossip, contention ceases." The point is the same: if you eliminate the fuel; the fire goes out.

If your passion for the Lord is flickering, then worship. You can go to YouTube and find thousands of worship songs. If it's with your wife that the fire is dwindling, find some fuel to re-ignite the flame. Especially in relationships, it's important to know the person's particular "love language." For example, if the love language of a person is "acts of service," then while giving that person a box of chocolates is not bad per se, it's not the right fuel. They would rather you clean the house or fix the broken door.

Just recently I wanted my wife to know that for no special reason she was important to me. We hadn't had a disagreement or conflict, so I wasn't bringing a peace offering. I thought I would just surprise her. I knew she was getting her nails done, so I decided to go and without her knowledge, pay the manicurist. Before I went though, I bought six roses and had them placed in little bottles so they wouldn't wilt before she brought them home. As I was trying to decide which flowers to buy, the young woman asked me if I needed help. I told her that I was looking for the freshest flowers.

In the course of the conversation I thought I would seize the opportunity to share with her the kingdom principle of putting wood on the fire. Somehow the question arose about whether the flowers were for a special occasion. I said no but added that after being married 46 years I still want to fulfill the scripture in Proverbs - "where there is no wood, the fire goes out."

You could see that it impacted her. When I dropped off the flowers and paid for Donna's nails, the opportunity to share arose once again. The woman working asked me if they were for an anniversary, to which

I replied, "No, I'm fulfilling the Proverb which says that where there is no wood, the fire goes out."

This kingdom principle also works during conflict when tempers escalate. Afterall, it takes two people to have an argument. So if both are acting and speaking foolishly, you can be pretty confident the result will be foolishness. I love Proverbs 20:3 which says, "It is honorable for a man to stop striving, since any fool can start a quarrel." (NKJV)

Forgiving, Releasing, and Blessing

It is one thing to know the scriptures but quite another to apply them. For example, when someone hurts you deeply, and I mean deeply, the idea of forgiving, releasing, and blessing that person is not the first thing on your mind. Nor is it when you're in such a dark place that it seems impossible to forgive the person who's hurt you, let alone go further to release and bless them.

I have sat in hundreds of counseling appointments only to hear horrific stories of abuse, hatred, rape, sodomy, and more. Normally the people subjected to such things come because their lives are miserable and they have no peace. Almost immediately I know the problem and also the solution.

Jesus spoke an entire parable about the unforgiving servant in Matthew 18. It is a story of one man who is forgiven and released from his great debt but is unwilling to forgive and release the person indebted to him. In verse 27 we read,

"Then the master of that servant was moved with compassion, released him, and forgave him the debt."

But... this deed is not reciprocated. Not by a long shot. Verses 18-30, "But that servant went out and found one of his fellow servants who owed him a hundred denarii; and he laid hands on him and took him by the throat, saying, 'Pay me what you owe!' So his fellow servant fell down at his feet and begged him, saying, 'Have patience with me, and I will pay you all.' And he would not, but went and threw him into prison till he should pay the debt."

When this is reported to the first land owner we see the repercussions of his not forgiving and releasing in verses 32-34, "Then his master, after he had called him, said to him, 'You wicked servant! I forgave you all that debt because you begged me. Should you not also have had compassion on your fellow servant, just as I had pity on you?' And his master was angry, and delivered him to the torturers until he should pay all that was due to him."

Did you see the word torturers? The Darby Translation, as well as other translations, use "tormentors." Jesus was saying that when a person doesn't forgive and release they can be tormented.

I knew this to be true in the situation where a drunk driver killed my brother. I forgave the woman but wanted her to pay by going to jail. Because of the way the evidence was collected, however, she wasn't convicted and was even released. For three years I was miserable because though I had forgiven her, I hadn't released her.

It's like when someone loans you money and at some point, they tell you that they'll forgive the debt, but every time you see them they remind you that they forgave it -- forgiven but not released.

We have a perfect example of how in the middle of extreme pain Jesus chose to forgive and release those who participated in his crucifixion. Luke 23:34 (NKJV): "Then Jesus said, 'Father, forgive them, for they do not know what they do.' "

The third step is to fulfill Luke 6:28, "Bless those who curse you." Bless them that they might truly know God.

If you wait for a feeling to forgive, release, and bless, the day may never come. But like Jesus in the middle of his agonizing pain, choose to forgive, release and bless (FRB). Yes, it is a choice. I have had people say they couldn't, to which I say, "Your Spirit wants to forgive, but your flesh is unwilling." I then have them pray, "Lord my flesh doesn't want to 'FRB,' but my Spirit does, so in the name of Jesus, from my Spirit I forgive, release, and bless."

I have never once seen a person who had been tormented not freed from it. Hebrews 4:12 (NKJV) says, "For the word of God is living and powerful, and sharper than any two-edged sword, piercing even to the division of soul and spirit, and of joints and marrow, and is a discerner of the thoughts and intents of the heart."

I Need Perspective

The past few days have been interesting. Yes, they've been interesting.

When things aren't going very well I think all of us can lose perspective. It's like seeing the White Mountains of New Hampshire turn into the Colorado Rockies. Then when things escalate I can begin feeling sorry for myself. I start getting the "why me's," which in turn affects my perspective on everything. It's like getting poked in the eye and everything becomes blurry. I can feel my peace being stolen and taken right away from me.

Let's see what happened. Instead of hitting "save" after writing the first 20 pages of my new book, for example, I hit "replace." The only thing saved were the 100 or so topics I wanted to cover in this new book. Then…my Google Pay account was hacked. This affected my personal bank accounts, and I needed new ones. These are in turn linked to my PayPal and credit card information. The bank representative said the situation created a ripple effect akin to throwing a pebble in a pond. I needed to change the usernames and passwords on several accounts. Thankfully all this was caught within ten hours, but oh what a mess. Even the few days before had had its own set of issues.

The temptation during such times is to entertain a complaining spirit. Thankfully I can hear the voice of God remind me of my choices: I can complain or I can celebrate. All the while He's trying to give me perspective. He shows me the faces of people I know going through "real issues/real problems," like the people in Redding, California losing their homes and businesses because of the fire. There are others facing betrayal, and still others with very serious health issues or those wondering where their next meal will come from. They have no electricity, no water, their everyday life literally about survival.

I can see Philippians 4:8 (ERV) in my mind, even though my natural/carnal mind doesn't want to acknowledge it: "Brothers and sisters, continue to think about what is good and worthy of praise. Think about what is true and honorable and right and pure and beautiful and respected." The battle rages in my mind, and my feelings join right in. He reminds me of Isaiah 26:3 (ISV): "You will keep perfectly peaceful the one whose mind remains focused on you, because he remains in you."

Finally, I come to the reality and the privilege of my role as an intercessor. I can think about the severity of things others are facing and can pray for them.

Yes, there is a battle in my mind, and I need perspective.

Complaining

So what's the big deal about a little complaining? After all, I'm only human. Or perhaps we can be honest and say we give ourselves permission to be carnal. By giving ourselves permission, we're deciding to allow the consequences of being carnal to enter our lives.

The Greek word translated "complainer" means literally "one who is discontented with his lot in life." It is akin to the word grumbler. Complaining is certainly not a fruit of the Spirit (Galatians 5:22-23) and in fact, is contrary to the peace, joy, and patience the Spirit provides.

How do you feel when you see/hear someone complain? Does it alienate you from wanting to be around this person? One minute we're talking to people about Jesus and their need for salvation. Then within the same dialogue-- the next hour, day, or week -- people can hear us complaining. Should we really be surprised when the person to whom we're trying to minister doesn't respond favorably to our talk about Jesus?

The Bible is full of examples about people grumbling and complaining. In fact, the first evidence of complaining in the Bible is in Genesis 3:12 when Adam complains about the woman God gave him. Then again, when the children of Israel are leaving Egypt, and as they continue their journey, all along the way they grumble and complain. Numbers 11:11 (NKJV) "Now when the people complained, it displeased the Lord; for the Lord heard it, and His anger was aroused. So the fire of the Lord burned among them, and consumed some in the outskirts of the camp."

Yup, complaining doesn't please the Lord. Have you ever noticed how you feel when you complain? Your peace is gone and you tend to be negative about everything.

God's admonition to us about complaining is extremely clear. Philippians 2:14 (EXB): "Do everything without complaining [grumbling] or arguing."

God spoke to me years ago and said that I could either complain or celebrate. I do my best to choose celebration. I'll leave you with these instructions from the Holy Spirit:

James 1:2-4 (NKJV): "My brethren, count it all joy when you fall into various trials, knowing that the testing of your faith produces patience. But let patience have its perfect work, that you may be perfect and complete, lacking nothing."

Saul

When you think of King Saul, what comes to mind?

What is common to most is how Saul treated David. In 1 Samuel 18:11 we read, "And Saul cast the spear, for he said, 'I will pin David to the wall!'" But David escaped his presence twice. Often when God allows a Saul in our lives, that person throws spears at us in the form of their words and behavior.

The Saul's in our lives are there for a reason. It's not so we can complain about them to God or to other people. More often it's about the Holy Spirit working certain things out of us and other things into us. The Saul's in our lives are God's appointed agents.

I had a pastor over me; he was a wonderful man and very anointed. Yet there were numerous times he became insecure and would misread, misunderstand, and misinterpret what I was doing. Also, there were many times that he wanted me to do unreasonable things. Since what he told me to do wasn't sin, I followed his instructions because it's important to have a centurion spirit.

Matthew 8:9: "For I also am a man under authority, having soldiers under me. And I say to this one, 'Go,' and he goes; and to another, 'Come,' and he comes; and to my servant, 'Do this,' and he does it."

The man would get angry and say things to me and to others that were very hurtful. I never reacted and always expressed myself very respectfully, never speaking about him to others. One day in my prayer for him I was telling God about his faults. God told me that there was "only one accuser of the brethren," and it wasn't me. He said he "wanted to work on me and not to worry about the pastor."

Here's something that it took me time to see, so I pray you can see it more quickly! It is that we can recognize the Saul in others but often fail to see the Saul inside ourselves. We must learn from David who served Saul with faithfulness and integrity. David understood that despite Saul's numerous flaws that God had appointed Saul as king and as someone to be over him. It is essential that we understand that God works through imperfect people, including ourselves.

I promise you that the day will come when you will be filled with gratitude that God allowed a Saul in your life.

Who Has the Problem?

Many times, when we have conflict with other people it's a result of a problem people have with us. The problem can be real, or it can be a misunderstanding, or even a total distortion of the truth.

When I realize that a person has a problem with me I ask the Holy Spirit to help me see, to take responsibility in the matter, and as needed, to have a willingness to change. This is particularly necessary when the strain in the relationship is obvious, when negative behaviors and attitudes are plain for all to see.

I ask myself whose problem it is. If it is the other person's, then I refuse to take their problem on board. If I react (instead of responding), I often escalate the problem. Proverbs 26:4 (EXB) is critical to live by: "Don't answer a fool according to his foolishness, or you will be just like him." The ERV says in verses 4-5, "There is no good way to answer fools when they say something stupid. If you answer them, then you, too, will look like a fool. If you don't answer them, they will think they are smart."

When we answer someone foolishly the result is two fools trying to resolve the problem. A video camera capturing the situation would reveal just how foolish we're both acting.

I'm willing to work through the problems others have with me, but in the process refuse to take on the attitudes associated with the conflict. Proverbs 29:11 says, "A fool vents all his feelings, but a wise man holds them back." (NKJV)

Who has the problem?

Worshipping When Everything Says Don't

How many times in your life have you been faced with tragedy or have been deeply hurt or wounded? In these circumstances have you felt like worshipping?

When all is well it's easy to worship, but in the midst of our pain, sorrow, and suffering worship doesn't come as naturally. I offer this to you as something to ponder.

2 Samuel 12:18-21 (NKJV): "Then on the seventh day it came to pass that the child died. And the servants of David were afraid to tell him that the child was dead. For they said, 'Indeed, while the child was alive, we spoke to him, and he would not heed our voice. How can we tell him that the child is dead? He may do some harm!' When David saw that his servants were whispering, David perceived that the child was dead. Therefore David said to his servants, 'Is the child dead?' And they said, 'He is dead' So David arose from the ground, washed and anointed himself, and changed his clothes; and he went into the house of the Lord and worshiped."

Imagine asking if your child is dead and hearing a yes response?

In the face of it, though, what David does is remarkable - He worships when everything says don't.

In Acts 16 we find a similar thing. Even though Paul and Silas are arrested, beaten, and put into prison, they do the same - they worship! It says in verse 23, "And when they had laid many stripes on them, they threw them into prison, commanding the jailer to keep them securely. Having received such a charge, he put them into the inner prison and fastened their feet in the stocks. But at midnight Paul and Silas were praying and singing hymns to God, and the prisoners were listening to them. Suddenly there was a great earthquake, so that the foundations of the prison were shaken; and immediately all the doors were opened and everyone's chains were loosed."

In the middle of physical and emotional pain Paul and Silas continued to pray and worship, even when everything said don't. Did you notice that people were watching them? People watch us as well.

When they chose worship the supernatural was released.

Can I/we worship when everything says don't?

When Your Day is from Hell

I wish we didn't have days that were surely designed by Satan himself. The days when everything goes wrong, when your whole life is turned upside down. You know, the days when you don't know you if you're going to make it through? These are days that we're all praying would come to an end or where we're wishing certain events hadn't happened.

In my 69 years of life and 48 years in the church, I've had a bunch of those days. Days when every breath hurts. Where I felt like Humpy Dumpty, "when all of the king's horses and all the king's men couldn't put Humpty Dumpty back together again." Days when I felt God had abandoned me. Days when I felt all alone. Days when the devil seemed to have more power than God. Days when I was so confused that it was nearly impossible to focus.

Days when I wasn't able to take every thought captive to the obedience of Christ even though I was told that God would enable me to do so. Second Corinthians 10:4-5 (NKJV): "For the weapons of our warfare are not [a]carnal but mighty in God for pulling down strongholds, casting down arguments and every high thing that exalts itself against the knowledge of God, bringing every thought into captivity to the obedience of Christ."

On these days I have to find something I can cling to. There are times when we're like the men who were going to Rome on the boat with Paul in Acts 27. There is a severe storm and they put cables around the ship to keep it together. And we have done likewise as we've looked for something to keep our lives together. We, like these men, feel that there is no way out of the storm and all hope is gone, verse 20, "Now when neither sun nor stars appeared for many days, and no small tempest beat on us, all hope that we would be saved was finally given up."

But Paul held onto what God had spoken to him, that he would arrive in Rome. Verses 23-25, "For there stood by me this night an angel of the God to whom I belong and whom I serve, 'Do not be afraid, Paul; you must be brought before Caesar; and indeed God has granted you all those who sail with you. Therefore take heart, men, for I believe God that it will be just as it was told me.' "

I can't tell you just how many times I've had to remind myself, others, the devil, and even God Himself, what God has spoken to me. I have had to fight everything - reality, emotions, you name it - with the prophetic words God has given me.

First Timothy 1:18 (NKJV): "This charge I commit to you, son Timothy, according to the prophecies previously made concerning you, that by them you may wage the good warfare." I have had to declare what God has said about my life and future. I've remembered Joseph in Genesis 39 when things went from bad to worse and "God was with him."

Then there is the verse in Romans that I think none of us like hearing when our lives are upside down. As much as I don't care to hear it when I am hurting, it's still true, and my feelings don't change the truth. Romans 8:28 (AMB): "And we know [with great confidence] that God [who is deeply concerned about us] causes all things to work together [as a plan] for good for those who love God, to those who are called according to His plan and purpose."

I'm Right

I came to sit before the Lord to be with him. I began to surf YouTube for new worship songs that I could experience with true sincerity. I sought to find a new song that could communicate things inside of me that I can't express on my own, because I wanted to sing words that would cause me to love Him even more.

I don't want to worship for the feeling (though I love the feeling), because worship is more than feeling good.

I read the following quote by CS Lewis, "Jesus didn't come to make bad people good but to make dead people alive!" I began to rejoice as these words penetrated my heart.

In the midst of rejoicing, I realized that I was this dead man who was made alive, not by what I have done, but solely on what he (Jesus) has done. God then reminded me of something He'd spoken to me years ago: "Dead men don't have rights." The moment we were baptized we entered our watery grave and were buried with Christ. Paul writes this in

Romans 6:4 (NKJV): "Therefore we were buried with Him through baptism into death, that just as Christ was raised from the dead by the glory of the Father, even so we also should walk in newness of life."

I could see times in my life and in the lives of others when we clung to being right, which meant that the other person was wrong and needed to change. In the moment I was blinded from seeing that, and so my need to be right produced an atmosphere of negativity, self-righteousness, and even hostility. It certainly affected my relationships. One day I heard the Lord say, "How is your being right working out for you?"

It wasn't. How is it working out for you?

As I considered these thoughts the parable from Luke 18:10-14 came to mind. It says, "Two men went up to the temple to pray, one a Pharisee and the other a tax collector. The Pharisee stood and prayed thus with himself, 'God, I thank You that I am not like other men—extortioners, unjust, adulterers, or even as this tax collector. I fast twice a week; I give tithes of all that I possess.' And the tax collector, standing afar off, would not so much as raise his eyes to heaven, but beat his breast, saying, 'God, be merciful to me a sinner!' I tell you, this man went down to his house justified rather than the other; for everyone who exalts himself will be humbled, and he who humbles himself will be exalted."

I'M RIGHT… Or am I?!

Who Is Serving Whom?

Imagine for a moment that you are God, and as much as you delight in the prayers of your people, you wonder why they pray the way they do.

It might be good to go back and see how Jesus said we should pray. He didn't mean for his words (in Matthew 6:5-13) to be said repetitiously - though this is not wrong - but instead to be a guide to prayer.

It's interesting to note the first thing Jesus says about praying. Here are verses seven and eight: "And when you pray, do not use vain repetitions as the heathen do. For they think that they will be heard for their many words. Therefore do not be like them. For your Father knows the things you have need of before you ask Him."

Jesus said that God is not obligated and furthermore doesn't listen to vain, repetitious prayers. But here is the key point, "For your Father knows the things you have need of before you ask Him."

So why is it that millions of Christians get up each day and tell God what to do, how to do it, and when to do it? And while it's not wrong to tell God the things on our heart, giving God His daily to-do list seems to be our main focus. Remember that He's already told us that He knows what we need before we even ask Him.

Think for a moment about how often we TELL God the need or problem even though He knows the matter far better than we do. Secondly, we ask and even tell Him how to fix or solve the problem when we don't really know what the real problem or need is. This amounts to millions of voices telling God how to do things! Thirdly, we often give God a time table, as in "I need an answer this week, tomorrow, or even today!"

Here is what Jesus said about prayer in Matthew 6:9-15 (NKJV): "In this manner, therefore, pray: 'Our Father in heaven, Hallowed be Your name.' " He's suggesting that we start our prayer with worship. And verse 10: "Your kingdom come. Your will be done on earth as it is in heaven." He does talk about our needs, but clearly, He's telling us to be focused on the Kingdom. We see this concept later in this chapter when Jesus says in verse 31-33: "Therefore do not worry, saying, 'What shall we eat?' or 'What shall we drink?' or 'What shall we wear?' For after all these things the Gentiles seek. For your heavenly Father knows that you need all these things. But seek first the kingdom of God and His righteousness, and all these things shall be added to you.' "

If we're Kingdom-minded then God tells us He'll give us the things we have need of. Then we see verse 11: "Give us this day our daily bread."

Jesus concludes how to pray with verses 12-15: "And forgive us our debts,

As we forgive our debtors. And do not lead us into temptation, but deliver us from the evil one. For if you forgive men their trespasses, your heavenly Father will also forgive you. But if you do not forgive men their trespasses, neither will your Father forgive your trespasses."

I'm not trying to cover the whole subject of prayer, but I would ask you to consider - WHO IS SERVING WHOM?

I Like Mercy for Me

Before you open your eyes in the morning, ponder this gem: His mercies (plural) are waiting for us.

In fact, in Lamentations (3:22-23 NKJV) it says, "Through the Lord's mercies we are not consumed, Because His compassions fail not. They are new every morning; Great is Your faithfulness."

I wonder if we have mercy for others every morning? As we open our eyes we're greeted by His love and affection, mercy and grace, and everything else freely available to us. Yes, even when life is upside down and we can't see a thing, His provision is there. But do we willingly have a heart to offer this same mercy and grace to others?

Just for a moment think about all the "stupid" things we do, say, and think. Psalm 103:10-11 in the Voice Bible says, "Thankfully, God does not punish us for our sins and depravity as we deserve. In His mercy, He tempers justice with peace. Measure how high heaven is above the earth; God's wide, loving, kind heart is greater for those who revere Him."

Yet how does this apply to people around us? If it's for me, then it's for them as well, even when at times I don't want it to apply to others because their actions have dramatically affected me.

Thankfully through all of it, we are no longer under the law but under grace. I am praying that I can treat others likewise. There are times when we're basking in mercy and grace ourselves but desiring law in our hearts and minds for others.

Perhaps we all can take some time and ask the Lord to help us consider His mercies, that they are new/fresh every morning. Here is

Lamentations 3:22-24 in the Amplified Bible: "It is because of the Lord's mercy and loving-kindness that we are not consumed, because His [tender] compassions fail not. They are new every morning; great and abundant is Your stability and faithfulness."

Lord help me want the same mercy for others.

If You Would Believe

Can we begin to allow the Holy Spirit to challenge us to step into a deeper dimension of believing?

There is so much more that is available to us, but our capacity to believe is impacted by what we see and also by what we don't. In other words, our eye sight and natural mind hinder and restrict us. It's kind of funny that we can believe for others but find it much more difficult to believe for ourselves.

Honestly, I can hear the Holy Spirit say, "Go ahead and believe me," adding, "Am I a liar?" The answer is in Hebrews 6:18 (NKJV): "It is impossible for God to lie." I can see that we have the faith to believe for the little things, but when it comes to bigger things... well, we just don't go there. We tend to hope but not believe. I hear again, "Go ahead and believe, you really have nothing to lose."

I began to write this because we (the church) are in desperate need to believe, to step into believing God for greater things. We have been too much like Gideon with the fleece in Judges 6 - make the fleece wet, no, make it dry.

The words of Jesus to Martha are ringing in my mind. Remember Lazarus has been dead for four days, and Jesus tells Martha to believe that he can raise Lazarus from the dead? What is in our lives that appears to be dead, where there is no appearance of life? What is it that the Holy Spirit is speaking to each of us about? What seems impossible?

John 11:40 (NKJV): "Jesus said to her, 'Did I not say to you that if you would believe you would see the glory of God?' " The meaning of this according to Gill's Commentary is: "wherein the glory of his power and goodness would be displayed, and the Son of God be glorified, or should see such a miracle wrought (resurrection of Lazarus). If we would believe we would see the power and goodness of God displayed for the whole world to see."

God is about to do the most amazing things. He's just looking for people through whom to do them. Jesus said, IF YOU (not someone else) WOULD BELIEVE - YOU, YOU, YOU WILL, WILL, WILL - SEE THE POWER AND GOODNESS OF GOD!

Wounded

When I came into the church years ago I had the idea that I wouldn't be hurt inside the walls of the church. I didn't stop and realize that the church is made up of imperfect people (including me) who God is still working on.

I have had the opportunity on a number of occasions to experience Zechariah 13:6 (NKJV): "I was wounded in the house of my friends." To be hurt by another person in the church is one thing, but to be wounded by a leader and in particular a pastor, is an entirely different story.

I remember in the early 1970s when the senior and associate pastors didn't like each other and would express their feelings about each other to me. After some time passed I told them they needed to work it out together. They sure did! They called a meeting with my wife Donna and myself, and all of a sudden, I was the bad guy.

I know when I have been hurt and deeply wounded, it takes maturity and determination to forgive and release the people who have hurt me. At these points it's helpful to be honest with myself and admit that I have done my own share of hurting others, both in and outside of the church.

How many times have we said or done things that have hurt other people? How many times have we repeated something that we shouldn't have repeated?

Proverbs 17:9 (NKJV): "He who covers a transgression seeks love, But he who repeats a matter separates friends."

Proverbs 10:19 (NKJV): "In the multitude of words sin is not lacking, But he who restrains his lips is wise."

Then there is this marvelous scripture that will help all of us from wounding others:

Proverbs 17:28 (NKJV): "Even a fool is counted wise when he holds his peace; When he shuts his lips, he is considered perceptive."

If you've been wounded, seek to forgive and release those you've wounded. If you have wounded, if possible seek out those you've hurt and ask for their forgiveness.

Remember that the church is made up of imperfect people who God is still working on (including you).

The Struggle for A Reputation

As a naturally-minded person you'd think that you should be concerned about your reputation. The natural man likes to be thought well of. He likes to be popular, and loves when he is exalted. He enjoys being a "somebody." Yet that is the natural man, not the spiritual one.

John the Baptist said in John 3:30 (NKJV), "He must increase, but I must decrease." John was saying, in effect, less of us and more of Jesus. When Samuel was speaking to Saul and explaining why God was taking the kingdom from him, he told him that he did well his first-year ruling as king but then began to be prideful (full of himself). Samuel told Saul that when he was small in his own eyes (when he saw himself as insignificant) that God raised him up to lead Israel.

First Samuel 15:17 says, "So Samuel said, 'When you were little in your own eyes, were you not head of the tribes of Israel? And did not the Lord anoint you king over Israel?' " Here in First Samuel you'll see that Saul was more concerned about his reputation than being accountable. Simply put, he wanted to look good in front of the people, yet sadly found that the more he tried to build a reputation, the further he got from God.

The subtle process of building a reputation takes time away from building God's Kingdom. A natural question follows: is it wrong to have a good reputation?

Good question, and two verses come to my mind: The first is Proverbs 27:21 (NKJV): "The refining pot is for silver and the furnace for gold, and a man is valued by what others say of him." The second is Philippians 2:7 (NKJV): "...but made Himself of no reputation, taking the form of a bondservant, and coming in the likeness of men." The "he" in this case is Jesus.

Being concerned about our reputation will keep us prisoner to people's opinions, and that will become our priority. Jesus said in John 8:29 (NKJV), "And He who sent Me is with Me. The Father has not left Me alone, for I always do those things that please Him." Jesus' focus was pleasing his Father, not people. Your reputation doesn't depend on what others say, and if it does, then you will be subject and vulnerable to all sorts of rumors, gossip, and ever-changing opinions.

End the struggle to have a reputation, and just enjoy being God's son or daughter!

The Coin

I have spent countless hours counseling people and have discovered that almost every problem or difficulty boils down to a simple matter of difference in perspective. Willingness is needed in order to see things from the lens of the other person.

If you take a quarter and hold it up between two people, one person sees a head and the other a tail. Who is right, you might ask. Who is telling the truth? The answer is, both are. Both people are thoroughly convinced that they are right, and they are!

Besides having a willing heart, what should we do? Let's look at Proverbs 2:3 (ICB): "Cry out for wisdom. Beg for understanding." We have to have a deep willingness to see another person's perspective. If we're unwilling to see then we'll remain blind and stubborn, and the unresolved conflict can become an issue that spills over into other areas of our lives. That's why we need to "cry out for wisdom and beg for understanding."

It's really not a matter of who's right, is it?!

Are Your Ears Painted On?

In the late 1990s I had the privilege of working with Pastor Glenn Feehan and his wife Robyn, also a pastor. Glenn and Robyn were from New Zealand and Australia, also known as "Down Under." Some of their expressions were so descriptive, one of my favorites being, "they have their ears painted on."

This expression describes people who are unwilling to hear and don't want to listen to input. They either refuse to listen or don't want to even consider the helpful counsel you're attempting to give.

Yes, their ears are painted on.

Are They Ready to Hear?

In the early years of my marriage and ministry I felt that if a person just understood my perspective or was exposed to another way of looking at something, then they would agree with me. Yet timing is everything. I can remember Donna saying, for example, "I don't want to talk about it right now."

Do you think I would respect her desire to talk about it later? No.

Many times in relationships one person is the communicator, and the other is not. One is comfortable with confrontation, and the other is not. One person is ready to talk, the other person puts off talking until later. One person is often a resolver and yet again, the other not.

People are in difficult places at times. They're angry, disappointed, frustrated, hurt, tired, etcetera, and they just don't have the capacity to hear what someone wants to say. And this is true of all of us sometimes– a conversation in the moment just seems impossible.

In the past I looked only at my needs or what I wanted and failed to see where the other person was at. It happens still now that I focus solely on my desires -- my need to talk, my need to try and to get people to see things my way and I'm thereby unable, or perhaps unwilling, to discern what is best for the other person.

There have been times when someone has held a certain view or conviction, and they're in a place where they sincerely don't even want to discuss or consider another view. They also can't understand why the matter even needs to be discussed right in that moment.

Isaiah 57:14 (NKJV) tells us, "Take the stumbling block out of the way of My people." Yet even while we are called to remove stumbling blocks, we can actually do the opposite and put them in another person's path. I think we've all been guilty of forcing a conversation, and when the other person doesn't respond well, we develop a wrong attitude. We blame the other person for their poor response, but in reality, the blame doesn't lie with them. The blame belongs to us, the provocateur.

Parents can be guilty of provoking their children but often resort to the excuse, "I'm the parent." Ephesians 6:4 (NKJV) says, "And you, fathers, do not provoke your children to wrath (anger)." Though the verse directly points to fathers, I believe the principle is true for all relationships.

Even Jesus understood that there are times that we shouldn't say anything. John 16:12 (TLB) says, "Oh, there is so much more I want to tell you, but you can't understand it now." Jesus knew that there is a time and season for everything. He was able to discern that there are times when people just can't hear. If Jesus knew there were times to speak up and times to be quiet, we should strive to be like him.

So, consider…are people ready to hear?

Learning to Be Content

Here in America people are obsessed with having "stuff." Then the rest of the world looks at America and wants "stuff" too. It's not wrong to have "stuff" (material things) as long as that stuff doesn't have YOU.

Unfortunately, even in the church people have forgotten the words of Jesus in Luke 12:15 (NKJV), "And He said to them, 'Take heed and beware of covetousness, for one's life does not consist in the abundance of the things he possesses.' "

People's desire to have more material things has served to rob them of being content. While it's not wrong to want to improve the conditions of our lives, when these desires end up stealing our peace, joy, and contentment, something is wrong. People's hunger for more natural/carnal things causes them to seek "things" rather than the Kingdom.

Jesus speaks about this in Matthew 6:25-33 (NKJV), "Therefore I say to you, do not worry about your life, what you will eat or what you will drink; nor about your body, what you will put on. Is not life more than food and the body more than clothing? Look at the birds of the air, for they neither sow nor reap nor gather into barns; yet your heavenly

Father feeds them. Are you not of more value than they? Which of you by worrying can add one cubit to his stature? So why do you worry about clothing? Consider the lilies of the field, how they grow: they neither toil nor spin; and yet I say to you that even Solomon in all his glory was not arrayed like one of these. Now if God so clothes the grass of the field, which today is, and tomorrow is thrown into the oven, will He not much more clothe you, O you of little faith? Therefore do not worry, saying, 'What shall we eat?' or 'What shall we drink?' or 'What shall we wear?' For after all these things the Gentiles seek. For your heavenly Father knows that you need all these things. But seek first the kingdom of God and His righteousness, and all these things shall be added to you."

Paul addresses the same thing in Romans 14:17 (NKJV), "For the kingdom of God is not eating and drinking, but righteousness and peace and joy in the Holy Spirit."

It's hard to imagine that we have the Kingdom and all its benefits yet are often still discontent.

I love what Paul writes in Philippians 4:11-12 (NKJV): "Not that I speak in regard to need, for I have learned in whatever state I am, to be content: I know how to be abased, and I know how to abound. Everywhere and in all things, I have learned both to be full and to be hungry, both to abound and to suffer need."

Did you notice the seven-letter word associated with the road to contentment? It's the word "learned." Paul implies that he too underwent a process to get to that place. It's not only learning to be content with where we are materially but also how to be content in our circumstances.

I spent a good part of my life wanting to be in a different place even spiritually, and it caused me to strive and not enjoy the moment. It's not wrong to hunger for more of the things of God but not to the point that we miss the joy of where we are and what God is doing in our lives. For example, for eleven years I was an associate pastor and for all of those I wanted to be in the senior position. My preoccupation with this had an effect not only on me, but also on my wife. I drove her nuts with wanting to be somewhere I wasn't. And yet it was a long time before I would be qualified to step up. Interestingly, when I was finally content where I was, God chose that particular time to release me into the senior position.

Honestly, due to discontent I lost years of enjoying the moment.

If I may plead with you, "learn to be content."

Say It

I grew up in a family that didn't say, "I love you" or express appreciation for what I had done or was doing. I was thus crippled in learning to express it to others.

All of us want to hear the Lord say to us, "Well done, good and faithful servant." We see this twice in Matthew 25:21&23 (NKJV). Yet what if we've never heard it ourselves?

Such cases are common. I know of many people who don't provide these words of affirmation, or for that matter other words expressing regret, sorrow, or wrongdoing. Yet the phrase "Jesus said" appears 124 times in the Bible. We see Jesus speaking to the Father and thanking him. Matthew 11:25 (NKJV): "At that time Jesus answered and said, 'I thank You, Father, Lord of heaven and earth, that You have hidden these things from the wise and prudent and have revealed them to babes.' "

In Proverbs 16:24 (NKJV) it says, "Pleasant words are like a honeycomb [liquid honey], making people happy and healthy [sweet to the taste and healing to the bones]." Proverbs 18:21 (TPT) says, "Your words are so powerful, that they will kill or give life."

Studies on children growing up in orphanages where they weren't spoken to or touched, support these points. One such study is found in Our Health, dated February 24, 2014, called "Orphans' Lonely Beginnings Reveal How Parents Shape A Child's Brain." In the article, Charles Nelson, a professor of pediatrics at Harvard Medical School and Boston Children's Hospital, says that there is more than a decade of research on children raised in institutions showing that "neglect is awful for the brain." Without a person who provides a reliable source of "attention, affection and stimulation," he says, "the wiring of the brain goes awry," the result being "long-term mental and emotional problems."

When people are not affirmed and validated it often causes them to lead a dysfunctional life. Not being loved in word or by touch, they often seek that validation and affirmation in unhealthy relationships.

When we don't "say it" we actually hurt people. We cripple them. We shape their lives, and not in a good way. Here is a promise that we must activate. Psalm 81:10 (NKJV): "I am the Lord your God, Who brought you out of the land of Egypt; Open your mouth wide, and I will fill it."

Yes, God has delivered us from our old lives where we were held captive, but now He has given us a new life and freedom. So if your argument is that you can't say it well, then you're going against scripture.

You can change lives with just a few words like, "I love you," "Good job," "I appreciate you," "Thank you," "I'm sorry," "I was wrong," or "Forgive me."

Go ahead...say it.

The I-Can't Anointing

Even though Philippians 4:13 (NKJV) says, "I can do all things through Christ who strengthens me," so often we really don't believe it. The Greek translation is, "I can do all things that God requires of me." Though this statement is perfectly clear, our natural mind has difficulty believing its simplicity and power. Whatever God requires of us He will enable and empower us to complete. He doesn't say it will be easy, but He does make it possible.

This concept of the I can't anointing is clearly displayed in the account of the Israelites approaching the promised land. As the children of Israel were poised to enter it, ten of the twelve spies saw the obstacles that existed as greater than the promise made to them about inheriting that land as a gift. Numbers 13:30-31 (NKJV) says, "Then Caleb quieted the people before Moses, and said, 'Let us go up at once and take possession, for we are well able to overcome it.' But the men who had gone up with him said, 'We are not able to go up against the people, for they are stronger than we.' "

It was said of Caleb that he had a different spirit. Numbers 14:24 (NKJV), "But My servant Caleb, because he has a different spirit in him and has followed Me fully, I will bring into the land where he went, and his descendants shall inherit it."

Sadly, the ten spies influenced approximately 2.5 million people to the degree that not one person besides Caleb and Joshua were able to enter. Because ten people said "We can't," the children of Israel spent the next 40 years wandering in the wilderness.

Having an "I can't" spirit prohibits people from enjoying everything that God has promised us. Can we see that our "I can't" spirit not only influences our own future but can hinder, limit, and prohibit other people as well?

We need the Spirit of Caleb who said in Numbers 13:30 (NKJV), "Let us go up at once and take possession, for we are well able to overcome it."

We must develop the I CAN SPIRIT…

Take A Ticket

When you go to the deli counter at the supermarket there's normally a line of people who are waiting to have their order processed. When you first arrive, you have to get a number from the ticket number dispenser so you'll know when you can be waited on.

What does all this relate to?

Numerous times there are people who feel quite free to express their opinion about what's going on in our lives. It's curious how often people have answers for someone else yet don't even have answers for themselves. It can be overwhelming, frustrating, and even angering to listen to people's unsolicited opinions and points of view, and often their influence creates confusion for us as to what we should or shouldn't be doing.

So before I get to the point of being angry or confused, I imagine myself directing people to the ticket dispenser. This way they need to wait in line along with everyone else who has an opinion. There are the rare times when even though I need to explain it to someone, I do advise people to, "Take a ticket."

It's at this point when we need to learn to respectfully say to people, "I love you, but you need to know I'm not looking for anyone's opinion or input but one, and He's not living on earth."

Don't be overwhelmed by people's opinions, just hand them a deli ticket, and they can stand in line just like everyone else.

Get Permission

I remember years ago standing in a line at a CVS pharmacy. There in front of me was a young woman in her late 20s. As I was standing there, the Holy Spirt began to speak to me about her life. The Lord was showing me that she and her husband were struggling in their marriage and they needed marriage counseling. As her order was filled and I was just stepping toward the pharmacy counter, I handed her my business card.

As she looked at my church business card I began to tell her what I had seen as she was standing in line. I told her that I was a pastor and that I saw that she and her husband were struggling in their marriage and desperately needed counseling. Without a word she threw my business card on the floor - and I mean threw - and literally ran out the door.

I learned a number of things that morning. Perhaps the biggest lesson was that I need to ask permission to share with people what I believe I'm seeing. Now when I see something about a stranger's life I approach them and say something to the effect of, "Excuse me. I was standing over there, and I believe the Lord spoke to me about your life. Would you like to know what He said?"

Using this approach, I have never had anyone tell me that didn't want me to share. In fact, there's often a look of anticipation on their faces.

What happens when I get their permission? It creates an openness to receive the word of God, similar to planting a seed on tilled, rather than untilled ground.

Get their permission…

Limiting God

Have you ever considered that at times we may be the ones who are limiting God from working in our lives and circumstances? All too often we blame the devil, when in reality it's not him, but instead, us.

We see this concept in Psalm 78:40-42 in the Passion Translation. It says, "How many times they rebelled in their desert days! How they grieved him with their grumblings. Again and again they limited God, preventing him from blessing them. Continually they turned back from him and provoked the Holy One of Israel! They forgot his great love, how he took them by his hand, and with redemption's kiss he delivered them from their enemies."

Do you see what it says? It points out that God's own children lived a lifestyle of grumbling and complaining, which in turn grieved the Holy Spirit. Does our grumbling and complaining grieve God? The answer is YES... In the case of the Israelites the text goes on to say that it PREVENTED God from blessing them.

What was the root of their grumbling and complaining? The root was that they forgot how much God loved them. They forgot that it was because of His love and affection that He delivered them from their enemies.

There is a second reason that God is limited from working in our lives - unbelief. If we recall, Jesus was visiting his hometown and was there limited as to what he could do. In Matthew 13:54 it says, "Jesus came to his home town" and then in verse 58 it says, "Now He did not do many mighty works there because of their unbelief."

If we're honest there are times in our lives that we too are faced with the reality of our unbelief. So what do we do? The first thing is to be honest with ourselves and the Lord and admit that we're struggling. We need to recall all the great things He has done in our lives. Then we need to ask the Lord for help. We see this principle in Mark chapter nine when Jesus is coming down from the Mount of Transfiguration and sees a boy who is demonized. Jesus asks the father of the boy a question, and then we can read the brief dialogue in verses 23 -24. Verse 23: "Jesus said to him, 'If you can believe, all things are possible to him who believes.' Immediately the father of the child cried out and said with tears, 'Lord, I believe; help my unbelief!' "

Let's be honest with ourselves and the Lord about the ways in which we're preventing God from working in our lives... The end of the story in Mark chapter nine says that once the father acknowledges his unbelief and asks for help, that Jesus immediately delivers the boy from Satan's control.

Jesus moves when we express our total dependence on him.

Here is another truth: many times, in spite of our unbelief and our grumbling and complaining attitude, God still works on our behalf.

Why? Because of His love for us.

Learn Well

I can't begin to tell you how many times God has allowed me to experience things that have been really hard, and at times it's seemed wrong and unfair. I can grumble and complain, but the truth is I can't imagine Jesus doing the same.

So why have all of us gone through struggles and trials? All that we've been through has been part of God's plan to equip and train us for His purposes.

Think about who you want to listen to in the middle of a trial. Is it somebody who's never been through trials or someone who has experienced the things you're going through? In Colossians 1:12 (NKJV) it says, "giving thanks to the Father who has qualified us to be partakers of the inheritance of the saints in the light." Yes, contextually we know that through the sacrifice of Jesus we have been qualified to be partakers of eternal life. Yet I also believe that God allows all of us to go through things to qualify us to minster to and comfort others when they experience similar trials.

This is clearly stated in 2 Corinthians 1:3-4 (Living Bible), "What a wonderful God we have—he is the Father of our Lord Jesus Christ, the source of every mercy, and the one who so wonderfully comforts and strengthens us in our hardships and trials. And why does he do this? So that when others are troubled, needing our sympathy and encouragement, we can pass on to them this same help and comfort God has given us." You and I go through things so we can be qualified to be more Christ-like and pour our lives into others.

I know when I am in the middle of trials, struggles, and very difficult and even painful times, I hear God say to me "LEARN WELL." What is He trying to tell me? First, if I learn well the first time it's less likely I'll have to go through the same thing again. Secondly, if I learn well I can truly be there for others when they go through similar trials. For this reason I can't tell you how many times I've thanked the Lord for allowing me to experience trials.

Whatever you go through - LEARN WELL... The day is coming when you'll be used by God to put your arm around somebody all because you're qualified firsthand to tell them that by God's unspeakable grace, they will make it through.

The song by Rita Springer says it well: "It's Going to be Worth It."

Having the Spirit of Ruth

In the Book of Ruth we find a woman by the same name who is the daughter-in-law of Naomi. Ruth leaves Moab to be with Naomi after Naomi moves back to Israel following the sudden death of her two sons. We are told that Naomi is a bitter woman. Yet in spite of that, Ruth wants to care for her.

Have you ever been around a bitter person for any length of time? It's not easy. Yet in spite of Naomi's bitterness, Ruth CARED FOR HER. As part of that caring Ruth would go into the harvest fields and find vegetables. It was practice then for harvesters to leave food behind for the widows.

In Ruth 2:7 Ruth asks permission to pick up the food that's been left behind. "And she said, 'Please let me glean and gather after the reapers among the sheaves.' So she came and has continued from morning until now, though she rested a little in the house." What a tremendous example for us to follow.

Notice what Boaz (the owner of the field), says about Ruth:

Ruth 2:11: "And Boaz answered and said to her, 'It has been fully reported to me, all that you have done for your mother-in-law since the death of your husband, and how you have left your father and your mother and the land of your birth, and have come to a people whom you did not know before. The Lord repay your work, and a full reward be given you by the Lord God of Israel, under whose wings you have come for refuge.' "

What an incredible reputation to have. What an incredible woman of God. Oh, that we would have the spirit that Ruth had.

There have been many times that I've told people that like Ruth, we must glean and gather when things are sparse, when there seems little or no anointing. To people who report scarcity, I say, "capture the anointing that is there." And by contrast in an environment where there is much, my response is to use all that's there.

I remember early in the 1990s being in an evangelical church to demonstrate how prophetic ministry is still viable. As usual there was worship which preceded the ministry time. That night although we sang songs; it really wasn't worship. Before we finished the last song, the pastor turned to tell me to start my ministry after we'd finished. As he turned back around I remarked to the Lord that "I couldn't find Him even if I had a flashlight." In other words, there was no anointing in the sanctuary.

Do you know what God said to me? He said, "If you don't carry the anointing, stay home."

I went to the pulpit having the Spirit of Ruth. I was going to glean what was there and not focus on what wasn't. It turned into a powerful night.

I pray that all of us would carry the Spirit of Ruth.

What You Do When the Brook Dries Up

In 1 Kings 17 we find the story of Elijah living by the Brook Cherith for three years because of the famine in Israel. For three years the ravens would bring Elijah his daily food provisions, while the brook provided his other basic needs.

Can you imagine what was going through Elijah's mind over the period of time that he watched the brook dry up? Since water is basic to sustaining life, Elijah has no choice but to move from his location. If the brook hadn't dried up, Elijah more than likely would have stayed where he was.

As in Elijah's life, sometimes God has to dry up our brook for change to come.

Many times the unique provision God has given in a certain season seems to disappear. This can include a steady job, good income, divine health, prophetic words, etcetera. Then, as with Elijah, the provision God has for you dries up. For example, you can be in a church for years which you really love. Then very suddenly you feel disconnected from the service. Where you were once encountering God, you now can't connect with Him. The church has a new pastor and you just can't relate to him or her. There could be dozens of other reasons, but the bottom line is "your brook has dried up."

When your brook dries up, as much as you don't want to, you know it's time to move. It's time for a change. This is a crucial moment in our walk with God. We must once again surrender our own will in order to receive His.

In Elijah's case, it meant traveling 100 miles to end up in Zarephath, which happens to be the home town of Jezebel (the woman/queen who was looking to kill him). Does it make any sense that God's provision is in Jezebel's hometown and that God uses a widow to provide a meal for him?!

When your brook dries up, know that it may be time to move. When it does, make sure you're not led by logic, but by the Holy Spirit.

The Kingdom is More Than Words

I can feel myself wanting to climb onto the roof of my home and shout with a clear and loud voice that the Kingdom of God is more than words. Why? Because I want everyone to know the truth of what Paul declared in 1 Corinthians 4:20 (NKJV), "For the kingdom of God is not in word but in power."

It is estimated that there are 320 billion "gods" worshipped on this earth. So why would people accept our religious/theological views over someone else's?

I believe Paul has the answer in 1 Corinthians 2:4-5 (NKJV): "And my speech and my preaching were not with persuasive words of human wisdom, but in demonstration of the Spirit and of power, that your faith should not be in the wisdom of men but in the power of God." There it is: we don't need persuasive words to demonstrate the power of God.

Jesus knew that in order to carry out the preaching of the gospel that the disciples would need to have a power beyond themselves. This is why Jesus insisted that the disciples stay in Jerusalem and wait for 50 days. We read this Acts 1:4-8: "And being assembled together with them, He commanded them not to depart from Jerusalem, but to wait for the Promise of the Father, which, He said, 'You have heard from Me; for John truly baptized with water, but you shall be baptized with the Holy Spirit not many days from now.' Therefore, when they had come together, they asked Him, saying, 'Lord, will You at this time restore the kingdom to Israel?' And He said to them, 'It is not for you to know times or seasons which the Father has put in His own authority. But you shall receive power when the Holy Spirit has come upon you; and you shall be witnesses to Me in Jerusalem, and in all Judea and Samaria, and to the end of the earth.' "

He wanted them to receive power so they could be witnesses.

Paul writes the church of Thessalonica in 1 Thessalonians 1:5 (NKJV) reminding them of what happened when he was there with them. Verse 5, "For our gospel did not come to you in word only, but also in power, and in the Holy Spirit and in much assurance, as you know what kind of men we were among you for your sake."

When I was in India visiting a village to share the gospel, I was asked to get up and preach but wondered why they'd listen to me when in India alone 33 million "gods" are worshipped. I went on to minister, believing that if the Kingdom of God was actually demonstrated, then they would listen.

I got up and began to pray for people, and the power of God manifested. In the end, in a village of 122 where only two were believers, by the time we had finished, about 80 people had committed their lives to the Lord.

The Kingdom is more than words…

The Three R's Plus One

We're looking for a way to thoroughly die to the sin in our lives so that it can no longer have power over us. If you remember that Jesus said he would give us the keys to the kingdom (Matthew 16:19, NKJV): "And I will give you the keys of the kingdom of heaven," the idea of keys carrying with it the idea of opening and closing, locking and unlocking.

I remember talking to the Lord many years ago about my need to change. He reminded me that change often comes when we repent. The idea of repenting reflects the concept of changing by going in the opposite direction, taking a 180-degree turn.

As I was musing with the Lord he spoke to me that 3 Rs are necessary in order to truly change.

First R - the need to recognize that there is a problem/sin

Second R - the need to take responsibility for the problem/sin

Third R - the need to repent

There is a fourth "R" which has to do with dealing with times in our lives when we've been involved with "curious arts" - witchcraft, fortune tellers, ouija boards, seances, and similar practices.

Fourth R - the need to renounce. We see the concept of renouncing in 2 Corinthians 4:2 (NKJV) where Paul writes, "But we have renounced the hidden things of shame" and in Acts 19:19 where people who were involved in magic (witchcraft) came and confessed their sin and burnt their books, verse 19 (NKJV), "Also, many of those who had practiced magic brought their books together and burned them in the sight of all."

The Greek meaning of renounce means to sever or to cut. The idea is that when we've practiced, dabbled in, or opened the door to the demonic realm in any way, even once, we need to close that door and disconnect from its influence. When we opened our lives to Jesus, He came in, and Satan can only copy what he sees God do.

In Revelation 22:15 we read, "But outside the city of God/heaven are dogs and sorcerers." The Greek word for sorcerer is "pharmakeia" which translated into "pharmacy," carries the idea of opening the door to witchcraft or spirits when people do drugs like marijuana, LSD, heroin, cocaine, etcetera. We establish a connection that remains open until we sever it, like the idea of an umbilical cord which has to be cut.

Thank God for the keys to the Kingdom.

Betrayal and Denial

One of the most painful and devastating things that can occur in your life is to be betrayed by someone close to you, to have someone you have poured your life into, deny you and fail to support you when you need it the most. It's easy to have a natural/carnal response to this, but we are not called to be naturally minded, but called to have the mind of Christ. What better example to have than Jesus.

Let's go to the evening of the last supper. It's such an incredible example of responding to betrayal. First, we see the way Jesus arranged the seating for the night. Peter is sitting in the servant's seat, and it will be his job to wash the feet of each guest. When Peter doesn't fulfill this responsibility, Jesus arises and during dinner washes everyone's feet.

In addition, later that night Peter will deny Jesus three times. The disciples fall asleep in the Garden of Gethsemane, and on the way to the garden have an argument about who will be the greatest – all in all, not a very good night.

Back to the last supper though… Peter is in the servant's seat and is angry and jealous about not sitting in one of the three seats of honor. The chief seat of honor is occupied by Jesus; John has the second seat, and the third seat of honor is occupied by Judas.

Think about this for a moment: you know already that you've been betrayed, and you're aware that in a short period of time you'll be arrested, scourged, and nailed to a tree. How would you feel towards your soon-to-be betrayer? What would your attitude be? Jesus, even knowing all these things, wanted to do everything he could to try and win Judas. Jesus' overwhelming, selfless love for Judas is also shown by him giving Judas the third seat of honor.

When Jesus comforts Peter about his denying him, he says, Luke 22:31-33 (Living Bible): "Simon, Simon, Satan has asked to have you, to sift you like wheat, but I have pleaded in prayer for you that your faith should not completely fail. So when you have repented and turned to me again, strengthen and build up the faith of your brothers."

Then after Jesus is raised from the dead he sends a special word to Peter. Mark 16:6-7 (NKJV): "But he said to them, 'Do not be alarmed. You seek Jesus of Nazareth, who was crucified. He is risen! He is not here. See the place where they laid Him. But go, tell His disciples—and Peter—that He is going before you into Galilee; there you will see Him, as He said to you.' " TELL PETER I'LL SEE HIM IN GALILEE…

I know this: Jesus has set an example for us to follow. 1 Peter 2:21 (NKJV): "For to this you were called, because Christ also suffered for us, leaving us an example, that you should follow His steps."

I am confident that even when we're betrayed and people fail to stand with us in our greatest moments of need, that we can still respond the way Jesus did.

Put Away Your Rocks

I had to learn to put away my rocks.

It's true that during the early years of my walk, I needed awareness that my opinion about other people's lives was just judgement in disguise. I still need to be aware, because it's common that when any of us sees or hear about something another person has done, we tend to sit in the judgment seat.

Years ago I was struggling with my attitude toward someone, and every time I saw them I'd only see their flaws. One day the Lord said to me, "Move over. You're sitting in my seat." I bowed my head in shame.

Within seconds the following verses flooded my mind:

Romans 14:4: "Who are you to judge (criticize/pass judgment) another's servant?"

Isaiah 51:1 (NKJV): "Look to the rock from which you were hewn, and to the hole of the pit from which you were dug." I needed to remember my journey, my flaws, my weaknesses. I had to remember where I came from.

John 8:3-5 (NKJV): "Then the scribes and Pharisees brought to Him a woman caught in adultery. And when they had set her in their midst, they said to Him, 'Teacher, this woman was caught in adultery, in the very act. Now Moses, in the law, commanded us that such should be stoned. But what do You say?'"

There's a Pharisee in each of us who tends to see things through the law, and thus carries around a pouch full of rocks. But Jesus sees things through his Father's eyes of mercy, grace, and forgiveness.

That's why Paul admonishes us in Philippians 2:5 (NKJV) to "Let this mind be in you which was also in Christ Jesus."

"Think as Christ Jesus thought." (NLV) Let's put away our rocks…

Stay Small

One of the greatest challenges is to have confidence and humility at the same time. Indeed, there's almost a divine tension between being confident in who we are yet not in what we do.

The tension exists because many of us struggle for approval and affirmation. We need someone to put their arm around us and say, "Good job." Our culture reinforces this at every turn, emphasizing performance, acknowledging and praising things well done. Over time this causes a performance addiction of sorts, the only way we can receive worth and value.

And yet, God says that my worth and value is not in what I do. It's in who I am.

When Jesus was baptized by John the Baptist, a voice spoke from heaven and said, "This is my son in whom I am well pleased." The voice didn't say, "This is the Messiah, who will soon save the world." Jesus' identity was not in what he did or was going to do, but in who he was. Grasping this reality has the potential to drastically change our lives.

The day will come when we'll realize that we aren't doing the work; it's the Spirit in us who's responsible. John 14:10 (NKJV): "Jesus said, 'But the Father who lives in Me does the work.'"

John the Baptist understood this principle - in order for the Spirit in us to increase, we need to get smaller. John 3:30 (NKJV): "He must increase, but I must decrease."

Samuel affirms this, telling Saul that he was successful when he was small in his own eyes. 1 Samuel 15:17 (Modern English Version): "Samuel said, 'When you were little in your own sight, were you not made the head of the tribes of Israel, and the Lord anointed you king over Israel?' "

Jeremiah 17:5 (NKJV) says, "Thus says the Lord 'Cursed is the man who trusts in man. And makes flesh his strength, whose heart departs from the Lord.' "

When we rely on ourselves and our ability, we stop putting our confidence in the Lord.

First Peter 5:5 provides the key to our remaining small: "Be clothed with humility."

Plans

I have to laugh. Most of us are able to quote Jeremiah 29:11 (TLB): "For I know the plans I have for you, says the Lord. They are plans for good and not for evil, to give you a future and a hope."

Funny though, that people have no idea what those plans are. If there are plans for us, wouldn't it make sense that we would know at least some of them?

I am fully persuaded that each of us has a very unique blueprint for our lives. Just now in writing this I see an office which belongs to an architect. The room is very dusty with cobwebs everywhere, and all over there are blueprints. Some are rolled up and have never been opened. Others are on drafting boards full of dust, because they haven't been looked at in a long time. Most of the open plans are on page one, and I hear that the plans have never been turned to page two, never mind to the pages which follow.

This means that many of us are stuck on page one and have never even turned the page to discover the rest of the plans...which brings me to a question. What has hindered us?

I see an older man who has a set of blueprints/plans in his hand. He's stretching his arm forward as if to give us the plans. "Take them," he seems to be saying. In fact, he's had his arm outstretched for quite some time. Can you hear him say - TAKE THEM?

" 'For I know the plans I have for you,' says the Lord."

The Entire Universe is Waiting for Us

My question is: do you recognize the following church?

Christ's Letter to the Church of Laodicea

"I know all that you do, and I know that you are neither frozen in apathy nor fervent with passion. How I wish you were either one or the other! But because you are neither cold nor hot, but lukewarm, I am about to spit you from my mouth." Revelation 3:15-16 (The Passion Translation)

Do you think that this is an accurate general description of the church today? You might say well, that's not my church, or perhaps it is. Either way, we're all part of the corporate church, so we might go on to ask if it's a description of us as individuals – not hot and not cold.

I keep on seeing Judges 15:4-5 (CEV): "Samson went out and caught three hundred foxes and tied them together in pairs with oil-soaked rags around their tails. Then Samson took the foxes into the Philistine wheat fields that were ready to be harvested. He set the rags on fire and let the foxes go. The wheat fields went up in flames, and so did the stacks of wheat that had already been cut. Even the Philistine vineyards and olive orchards burned." God wants to set us on fire so that He can send us into the fields of the world and spread the fire wherever we go.

I also keep hearing 2 Timothy 1:6 (AMPC): "That is why I would remind you to stir up (rekindle the embers of, fan the flame of, and keep burning) the [gracious] gift of God, [the inner fire] that is in you."

Very often we're asking God to rekindle the fire that was once in us when what He's really saying is, "Restart your own fire."

Can't you see? Can't you hear? Romans 8:19 (TPT): "The entire universe is standing on tiptoe, yearning to see the unveiling of God's glorious sons and daughters."

Have you seen the church of Laodicea? Have you seen the fields God wants you to set on fire? Can you see the fire already in you that needs to be rekindled?

Yes, the entire universe is waiting for us.

Write the Vision

Most of us are familiar with the scripture in Habakkuk 2:2 (ESV) which says, "And the Lord answered me: 'Write the vision; make it plain on tablets, so he may run who reads it.' "

It seems pretty clear that Habakkuk was told to write the vision that God was going to give him. Like him, we too need to take the time to write what God speaks to us. If I were to ask you if you had written the vision God has given you, what would your response be?

The verse continues to say, "Make it plain." In other words, don't make it so spiritual that it doesn't really make sense. On the other hand, don't make it so general that it's like a one-size-fits-all pair of socks, appropriate for anyone.

The third thing in the verse is that after you finish writing and reading it, you should be inspired to activate the word you've been given. The word used in the verse is "run."

Here's a question. How many of us write the vision, make it clear, and then RUN?

Do you know why people don't write what they believe they're hearing from the Lord? Perhaps the biggest reason is that they don't want to be wrong. And if a person writes something, they only write what they have faith for. For example, the Lord may say, "You'll travel the world," but they write, "I am to travel." Or God says, "One day you'll have your own church," but their "translation" says, "God has called me to be a leader, and I will have an important role in the church."

I want to encourage you to WRITE YOUR VISION… Write it all down even though it might not make sense or seem possible. There is, after all, Luke 1:37 (NKJV): "For with God nothing will be impossible."

You might say that's true, "nothing is impossible" for God, BUT…

At this point there's also Matthew 17:20 (NKJV): "I say to you, if you have faith as a mustard seed, you will say to this mountain, 'Move from here to there,' and it will move; and nothing will be impossible for you." Take a moment and say this to yourself, "Nothing will be impossible for you."

What if all of us take a new step of faith? Start with writing your vision.

The Issue of Anger

Do our public and private lives look the same? Are we the same person at work as we are in church? How about the same person at home as at church?

A factor that can differentiate our public and private realms is our expression of anger, an area of huge struggle for a lot of people. And many believers don't really understand the difference between righteous and carnal anger.

If we're honest, there are few circumstances that can be attributed to righteous anger. Instead, most of our anger is due to a lack of patience or self-control, feeling disrespected (at least in our minds), frustration, annoyance, and plain bad days. Psychologists weighing in on the topic say that the primary reason for anger is past hurt.

Regardless of the reason, when people carry anger they often become so self-absorbed as to not see how they're affecting the lives of those around them.

Often when I'm ministering to pastors and leaders I tell them that they can't afford to have a bad day. When they do, like anyone else, they hurt people, and yet because of their position, the effect is greater.

James tells us that when people are angry it doesn't fulfill the purposes of God. James 1:20: "for the wrath of man does not produce the righteousness of God." The Passion Bible says, "for human anger is never a legitimate tool to promote God's righteous purpose." Indeed, when we're angry it can create a stumbling block for others.

Ephesians 2:26 (TLB) says, "Don't get so angry that you sin. Don't go to bed angry." The reality is that if we go to bed angry, we'll wake up angry. And even if we're not aware that we're angry, it doesn't mean the anger has disappeared. If the issue hasn't been resolved, that anger is dormant, and it won't take much for it to manifest. The result is that the anger's expression is often misdirected, and the anger is displaced.

One constructive expression of anger is through good communication that directly addresses the issue that provoked you in the first place. For example, a person borrows your car and then isn't paying attention. They get in an accident and cause a lot of damage. Instead of expressing anger through your flesh, it would be better to say, "I'm glad you're okay, but I'm angry that you weren't paying attention." Or... one of your children does something that upsets you. You can say to them, "Sweetheart, daddy loves you, but you have to know I'm angry. We'll work through this."

"Don't get so angry that you sin..."

Increasing Your Anointing

So often I'm asked by people to pray that their anointing would increase or as in the case of Elisha, to pray for a "double portion" of their anointing. Yet it's not often that I'll do it. Why?

Here are four principles that I think we need to look at:

The first is using the anointing that we have now. Why would God give us more if we're not using what we've already been given? Paul makes three points about this in Romans chapter 12: one, use what you have according to the level of faith that you have, and also, don't have a false perspective of your gifting/anointing (or don't see yourself as bigger than you are). Romans 12:3-8 (NKJV) is self-explanatory, "For I say, through the grace given to me, to everyone who is among you, not to think of himself more highly than he ought to think, but to think soberly, as God has dealt to each one a measure of faith. For as we have many members in one body, but all the members do not have the same function, so we, being many, are one body in Christ, and individually members of one another. Having then gifts differing according to the grace that is given to us, let us use them: if prophecy, let us prophesy in proportion to our faith; or ministry, let us use it in our ministering; he who teaches, in teaching; he who exhorts, in exhortation; he who gives, with liberality; he who leads, with diligence; he who shows mercy, with cheerfulness." With a spirit of humility use the gift you have with the level of faith that you have.

The second thing we need to look at is perhaps more difficult to embrace. Luke 16:10-12 (NKJV): "He who is faithful in what is least is faithful also in much; and he who is unjust in what is least is unjust also in much. Therefore if you have not been faithful in the unrighteous mammon, who will commit to your trust the true riches? And if you have not been faithful in what is another man's, who will give you what is your own?"

So when people are looking for more anointing or are frustrated because they seem to be restricted in functioning in the one(s) they have, perhaps they need to look at these verses.

Further, if you and I are not faithful with God's money, it tells us that we can't even receive what belongs to us already.

There are three keys to increasing the anointing on our lives: humility, using what we have at the level of faith we have, and being faithful with God's money.

He is the God of the Mountains and the God of the Valleys

In 1 Kings 20 we once again find Syria coming to attack an outnumbered Israel. King Ahab is still king of Israel, and he still doesn't honor or obey God. Yet because of God's deep love and affection for His people and the continual arrogance of the Kings of Syria towards God, God delivers Israel.

I am so thankful for our Father's unconditional love for us even when we aren't in a good place.

In verse 28 we see the arrogance of King Ben-Hadad and God's response to his arrogance: "A man of God came to the king of Israel with this message: 'The Lord said, "The people of Aram said that I, the Lord, am a god of the mountains and not a god of the valleys." So I will let you defeat this great army. Then all of you will know that I am the Lord, wherever you are!' "

Yes, our God is the God of the mountains and valleys, not only literally but spiritually. Whether we are on top of the mountains or in our lowest valley, our God is ever there for us.

I keep playing yesterday's worship song over and over again - "I will never be alone." When you find a song or a scripture that ministers to you, don't just run off to the next song or verse, let that song or verse saturate you.

He is the God of the mountains and the God of the Valleys, and in those places, we will never be alone. I believe the Holy Spirit is trying to do something in us. Stay here awhile, ponder, and worship.

Rise Up, My Fair One

I am sitting here in my office with tears in my eyes. I can see Jesus standing on a sloping mountain and his voice is echoing through the valley below. He's calling out with tears and trembling in his voice, "Rise up and come away. You still don't understand who you really are."

"If my sons and daughters could really believe that the same spirit that raised me from the dead lives in them." Can we hear Paul from Ephesians 1:19-20 (The Passion Translation): "I pray that you will continually experience the immeasurable greatness of God's power made available to you through faith. Then your lives will be an advertisement of this immense power as it works through you! This is the mighty power that was released when God raised Christ from the dead and exalted him to the place of highest honor and supreme authority in the heavenly realm!"

Can we whisper and then shout Psalm 139:14 (NKJV): "I will praise You, for I am fearfully and wonderfully made." In Titus and First Peter it says we are his special people, and several times in the Old Testament He calls us "His special treasure." Exodus 19:5 says, "You shall be a special treasure to Me above all people; for all the earth is Mine."

Within each of us is untapped potential. We have to stop looking at ourselves with our own eyes and see ourselves and others through His eyes. Oh Jesus, help us see.

There is a voice I can hear like one echoing through a canyon. "Can't you see who you really? YOU ARE MY SPECIAL TREASURE…"

Rise up, my love…

Lessons from the Valleys

The Valley of Berachah

There are 4290 valleys in the Bible, and today we're going to travel to the Valley of Berachah, or translated, Valley of Blessing. I am so excited about this valley, because it's not the valley where we're blessed, but is instead the valley where we bless God.

You might remember that in 2 Chronicles 20, Jehoshaphat is surrounded by a multitude of armies. There's no natural way that he can possibly win. Ever been there? You know all the times in our lives where there seems to be no way, but our Father makes one for us?

In the account, Jehoshaphat cries out to the Lord, and the prophet comes and tells him what to do in order to win. Turns out that the way to victory was through worship. 2 Chronicles 2:21-22 (ERV): "Jehoshaphat encouraged the men and gave them instructions. Then he had the Temple singers stand up in their special clothes to praise the Lord. They marched in front of the army and sang, 'Give thanks to the Lord! His faithful love will last forever.' As they began to sing and to praise God, the Lord set an ambush for the army from Ammon, Moab, and Mount Seir who had come to attack Judah. The enemy was defeated!"

Worshipping before battle is key, but is equally as important after. Here is the example:

2 Chronicles 20:25-26 (NKJV): "When Jehoshaphat and his people came to take away their spoil, they found among them an abundance of valuables on the dead bodies, and precious jewelry, which they stripped off for themselves, more than they could carry away; and they were three days gathering the spoil because there was so much. And on the fourth day they assembled in the Valley of Berachah, for there they blessed the Lord; therefore the name of that place was called The Valley of Berachah until this day."

We must continually travel to the Valley of Berachah (Blessing). Take a moment right now...

Welcome to The Valley of Aijalon

Oh Lord, lead us to the Valley of Aijalon...

This Valley is just outside the city of Aijalon which is now a city called Yalo, a little to the north of the Jaffa road, about 14 miles from Jerusalem.

This is the valley where miracles occurred. We find this valley in Joshua chapter ten as the Gibeonites hear about God defeating Jericho and Ai, and out of fear make a treaty with Israel.

Shortly after the treaty is enacted, five kings of the Amorites decide to go and attack Gibeon. As they come to make war with the Gibeonites, the king Gibeon sends word to Joshua to come and honor his treaty. Joshua 10:6: "And the men of Gibeon sent to Joshua at the camp at Gilgal, saying, 'Do not forsake your servants; come up to us quickly, save us and help us, for all the kings of the Amorites who dwell in the mountains have gathered together against us.' "

So Joshua is given the following instructions by God. Joshua 10:8-11: "And the Lord said to Joshua, 'Do not fear them, for I have delivered them into your hand; not a man of them shall stand before you.' Joshua therefore came upon them suddenly, having marched all night from Gilgal. So the Lord routed them before Israel, killed them with a great slaughter at Gibeon, chased them along the road that goes to Beth Horon, and struck them down as far as Azekah and Makkedah. And it happened, as they fled before Israel and were on the descent of Beth Horon, that the Lord cast down large hailstones from heaven on them as far as Azekah, and they died. There were more who died from the hailstones than the children of Israel killed with the sword."

You can't help but get excited about the fact that before we go to war, before we fight any battle, we've already won. Notice that we need to do our part, which will require some major effort at times (exemplified by their marching all night from Gilgal). But the Lord will step in for us as He did for them.

As they're fighting "the Lord cast down large hailstones from heaven on them as far as Azekah, and they died. There were more who died from the hailstones than the children of Israel killed with the sword." (Joshua 10:11)

If that wasn't enough, when Joshua comes to the Valley of Aijalon, he speaks to the sun and the moon. Imagine the power in our mouths. Here is what is written in Joshua 10:12-14: "Then Joshua spoke to the Lord in the day when the Lord delivered up the Amorites before the children of Israel, and he said in the sight of Israel: 'Sun, stand still over

Gibeon; And Moon, in the Valley of Aijalon.' So the sun stood still, And the moon stopped, Till the people had revenge Upon their enemies. Is this not written in the Book of Jashar? So the sun stood still in the midst of heaven, and did not hasten to go down for about a whole day. And there has been no day like that, before it or after it, that the Lord heeded the voice of a man; for the Lord fought for Israel."

Did you see that? "The Lord heeded the voice of a man; for the Lord fought for Israel." That is how much we are loved and how much God is for us. We see this affirmed in Daniel 10:12 (NKJV): "Then he said to me, 'Do not fear, Daniel, for from the first day that you set your heart to understand, and to humble yourself before your God, your words were heard; and I have come because of your words.' "

If you're still sitting in your chair I would be surprised... Let's go down to the Valley of Aijalon and see what miraculous things God will do for us...

Oh Lord, you are beyond any words I can utter. All I can do is lift my hands and worship.

Welcome to the Valley of Aijalon...

We Must Go Down to the Valley of Kidron

Six times in the Bible we see Israel destroying their idols by the Brook Kidron in the valley of the same name, now called the Valley of Jehoshaphat. It's the area just outside the east wall in the city of Jerusalem, between Jerusalem and the Mount of Olives. The Valley of Kidron is both large and deep.

While "Valley of Kidron" can have many meanings, I want to focus on the one concerning tearing down and destroying idols. The definition of idolatry, according to Webster, is "the worship of idols or excessive devotion to, or reverence for some person or thing." An idol is anything that replaces the one, true God or anything we value or honor more than the Lord. The most prevalent form of idolatry in biblical times was the worship of images that were thought to embody the various pagan deities.

So here's the question: what or who do we value or honor more than God? What comes immediately to mind are opinions and actions we put above the heart of God and His word. Many on their journey read certain scriptures and fail to accept them or choose not to acknowledge them because it's inconvenient, too hard, or they just don't want to. I have often called this "SHOPPING CART CHRISTIANITY," like a person in a supermarket traversing the various aisles and only putting in what they want.

The idols we serve are varied and may include our theology (not biblical theology), actions, feelings, opinions, etcetera. In 1 Kings 15:9-14 we read about King Asa: "In the twentieth year of Jeroboam king of Israel, Asa became king over Judah. And he reigned forty-one years in Jerusalem. His grandmother's name was Maachah the granddaughter of Abishalom. Asa did what was right in the eyes of the Lord, as did his father David. And he banished the perverted persons from the land, and removed all the idols that his fathers had made. Also he removed Maachah his grandmother from being queen mother, because she had made an obscene image of Asherah. And Asa cut down her obscene image and burned it by the Brook Kidron. But the high places were not removed. Nevertheless, Asa's heart was loyal to the Lord all his days."

While Asa tore down a lot of idols, the high places remained. Allowing these to remain eventually cost him his life. We can do this too: tear down the easy idols but leave the high places in our lives.

In 2 Kings 23:3-4 we read, "Then the king (Josiah) stood by a pillar and made a covenant before the Lord, to follow the Lord and to keep His commandments and His testimonies and His statutes, with all his heart and all his soul, to perform the words of this covenant that were written in this book. And all the people took a stand for the covenant. And the king commanded Hilkiah the high priest, the priests of the second order, and the doorkeepers, to bring out of the temple of the Lord all the articles that were made for Baal, for Asherah, and for all [b]the host of heaven; and he burned them outside Jerusalem in the fields of Kidron, and carried their ashes to Bethel."

Did you notice that in order to tear down and destroy their idols Josiah made a commitment? The word says that he "made a covenant before the Lord, to follow the Lord and to keep His commandments and His testimonies and His statutes, with all his heart and all his soul, to perform the words of this covenant that were written in this book." As with Josiah, for us to do likewise will require a total commitment.

If you aren't ready to do this, ask the Lord to change your heart.

Is the Spirit showing you that you need to go down to the Valley of Kidron?

The Valley of Eshcol

Remember God's promise at the burning bush that He would bring Israel out of the place where they were oppressed and into a land of milk and honey? Exodus 3:7-8: "And the Lord said: 'I surely seen the oppression of My people who are in Egypt, and have heard their cry because of their taskmasters, for I know their sorrows. So I have come down to deliver them out of the hand of the Egyptians, and to bring them up from that land to a good and large land, to a land flowing with milk and honey, to the place of the Canaanites and the Hittites and the Amorites and the Perizzites and the Hivites and the Jebusites.' "

It's important to note that God was honest with Israel that although several "ites" were there, he would bring them there safely and give them the land. The fulfillment of His promise came a bit later. Meanwhile Moses sends twelve spies into the promised land. In Numbers 13:1-2 we read, "And the Lord spoke to Moses, saying, 'Send men to spy out the land of Canaan, which I am giving to the children of Israel.' "

So Moses sends them to spy out the land for 40 days. In Numbers 13:23 it says, "Then they came to the Valley of Eshcol, and there cut down a branch with one cluster of grapes; they carried it between two of them on a pole."

While they found in the Valley of Eschol a place of divine and overflowing provision, there were obstacles in the land. Numbers 13:26-29: "Now they departed and came back to Moses and Aaron and all the congregation of the children of Israel in the Wilderness of Paran, at Kadesh; they brought back word to them and to all the congregation, and showed them the fruit of the land. Then they told him, and said: 'We went to the land where you sent us. It truly flows with milk and honey, and this is its fruit. Nevertheless the people who dwell in the land are strong; the cities are fortified and very large; moreover we saw the descendants of Anak there. The Amalekites dwell in the land of the

South; the Hittites, the Jebusites, and the Amorites dwell in the mountains; and the Canaanites dwell by the sea and along the banks of the Jordan.' "

The Valley of Eshcol is the valley where we need to decide our focus. We can see the overwhelming, supernatural provision of God (the fulfillment of His promises), or we can see the "ites," or the very real obstacles that exist.

So what is your focus? Do you see what God wants to do for you, or are the obstacles greater than God? What the Israelites chose to see were the obstacles rather than the supernatural provision that was already waiting for them.

How about you?

The Valley of Eshcol is a place where we're given a choice of what to see and embrace. Are you in this valley now? If not, you soon will be ... Make up your mind now what you're going to see...

Let's Go Down to the Valley of Dry Bones

This morning when I awoke I wasn't up three minutes when I was wondering what valley I would write about. Then immediately I heard, "the Valley of Dry Bones."

I knew exactly where to go as I opened my computer to Ezekiel 37. As I started reading my eyes filled with tears and my heart leapt, and even now as I write this I have such excitement in me. My eyes are watering, and I want to jump up in the hotel lobby and shout - GOD'S ABOUT TO DO SOMETHING...

In the first few verses in Ezekiel it says the Spirit of God brought Ezekiel down to the Valley of Dry Bones. Can we hear that God is visiting the Valley of Dry Bones? In verse 11 God speaks to Ezekiel and says, "Then He said to me, 'Son of man, these bones are the whole house of Israel. They indeed say, 'Our bones are dry, our hope is lost, and we ourselves are cut off.' "

As I look at the church I can identify with what God is seeing. The church in general is dry and in need of God's breath. There is so much hopelessness in the lives of so many and a sense of being lost in respect to both vision and purpose. Each day is like the day before where there is very little, if any expectation or joy that today we could see God move and that He wants to work through us.

Perhaps like Ezekiel we will prophesy, or breathe life.

In Ezekiel 37:7 (NKJV) it says, "So I prophesied as I was commanded; and as I prophesied, there was a noise, and suddenly a rattling; and the bones came together, bone to bone."

Did you see that? There was a noise, a rattling! Because Ezekiel prophesied, something incredible and supernatural happened. You too have this power to speak life. Remember the verse about the power of life and death being in the tongue (Proverbs 18:21)? Perhaps today God will show you someone who needs one or two words that bring encouragement. I'm not saying to give them deep revelation but one or two words that can encourage their heart, their soul. Perhaps it will come through delivering a hug or a smile? Go ahead, prophesy. In fact, in Revelation 10:11 it says, "You must prophesy."

As I'm writing I am so excited - GOD'S ABOUT TO DO SOMETHING... He wants to do something through you. He has brought us to this valley to show us that we are to breathe life. In verse 10 we see Ezekiel is commanded to prophesy again, "So I prophesied as He commanded me, and breath came into them, and they lived, and stood upon their feet, an exceedingly great army."

That's it - God is raising up an army, an army that's alive and carrying His presence wherever they go. That's YOU!

In verse three God asks Ezekiel this question, "Son of man, can these bones live?"

Jump up and yell – YES, THEY CAN!

The Valley of the Shadow of Death

Psalm 23:4 (NKJV) says, "Yea, though I walk through the valley of the shadow of death, I will fear no evil; For You are with me; Your rod and Your staff, they comfort me."

The Hebrew phrase for "shadow of death" is used in a poetic sense for thick darkness. Figuratively it means a place of deep distress. In Job 10: 21 & 22 it's the description of a place called Sheol.

This valley is a place where we in such deep despair and hopelessness that we're unsure if emotionally we're going to survive. There are moments here where it's hard to even take a breath. We feel like we want to die, or are so broken that we almost want to die. We feel desperately alone and don't know what tomorrow will bring.

We've all been there.

It's in this place of deep darkness and distress that David's Psalm gives us the insight we need to cling to. It's important to understand that we're only walking through the valley; it is not our permanent residence. We WILL make it out.

David declares that he will not fear. When we are in this valley, fear is our number one enemy. But we must not allow fear to overtake us but instead say with a loud voice, "I WILL NOT FEAR."

Why can we declare this? Because He is our shepherd, the shepherd who will be with us through everything that life brings our way. Yes, even in the deepest darkness and despair the Lord says to us, "FOR I AM WITH YOU." You might not feel it, but the truth is that we are NEVER, EVER ALONE. His rod (his ability to protect us) and staff (his ability to lead us) will never waver.

David knew as an earthly shepherd that God was his own heavenly shepherd, which is why he began his psalm that way. David knew that God, as a faithful shepherd, would always provide what was needed for his journey.

When everything has flooded our lives, and we feel like we're walking through hades (hell), our GOD IS THERE. So many times I've had to remind myself, "I am only passing through this valley."

Yes, it's another valley that we've all visited and one that in all likelihood we'll pass through again. I can't begin to recount all the times I've been here and have had to remind myself what He's said - "I AM WITH YOU."

He didn't say, "Maybe I will be with you." He said, "I am with you."

In the Valley of Elah

You are all familiar with this valley. It's the valley where we get to face our giants as did David when he defeated Goliath. There are some very important things to learn here.

First, David was told by his older brother that his heart was wrong; that he only came to see the battle or to be a bystander. Is this a familiar message from family, friends, and others? First Samuel 17:28 reads, "Now Eliab his oldest brother heard when (David) spoke to the men; and Eliab's anger was aroused against David, and he said, 'Why did you come down here? And with whom have you left those few sheep in the wilderness? I know your pride and the insolence of your heart, for you have come down to see the battle.' "

As a result, Saul fails to recognize his anointing and his potential. Ever been there? When people don't see who you are? When we're in this place it's important to hold fast to what and who we believe we are. Verse 33: "And Saul said to David, 'You are not able to go against this Philistine to fight with him; for you are a youth, and he a man of war from his youth.' "

David had a confidence that because God had delivered him in the past, He would deliver him again. Verse 37: "Moreover David said, 'The Lord, who delivered me from the paw of the lion and from the paw of the bear, He will deliver me from the hand of this Philistine.' " Never forget that no matter how big the obstacle, God will deliver you. All those small battles you've been in are to prepare you for bigger ones.

It's important to note that David used a supernatural means of defeating Goliath. Too often we rely on ourselves and our own abilities, but David relied on five stones which he'd pulled from a brook. We forget 2 Corinthians 10:4 (NKJV): "For the weapons of our warfare are not carnal but mighty in God for pulling down strongholds." Why is it that when we're facing our giants we look to a natural way of doing things? Think about it -- we rely on the natural to defeat something spiritual. It's like bringing a water gun to battle. As David defeated his giant in the Valley of Elah, you too can defeat your giant(s).

Did you ever wonder where everyone else was in the midst of this? The fact is that they stayed on the mountain, too afraid to face the giant. Perhaps we need to be willing to leave what we perceive as a safe place and actually go down to the valley.

Go ahead -- face your GIANT...

The Valley of Achor

Welcome to another valley. This time we're discussing the Valley of Achor (trouble), an area near Jericho. This is where Achan created the gold idols, which in turn caused Israel to be defeated in combat.

All of us have been here, but you're about to see how our God redeems and restores us when we're in this place.

In Isaiah 65:10 the people of God found provision not only for their sheep and cattle to lie down, but here in this valley of trouble the people who sought Him enjoyed His presence. From trouble they go all the way to blessings, rest, and God's presence. Isaiah 65:9-10 (AMPC): "And I will bring forth an offspring from Jacob, and from Judah an inheritor of My mountains; My chosen and elect will inherit it, and My servants will dwell there. And [the plain of] Sharon shall be a pasture and fold for flocks, and the Valley of Achor a place for herds to lie down, for My people who seek Me, inquire of Me, and require Me [by right of their necessity and by right of My invitation]."

Can we take this in? In the Valley of Trouble - which had been a place of calamity – there would come blessing. Yes, God can take out us out of trouble and calamity and cause the very same place to be one of rest and His presence.

If that isn't encouraging enough, then in Hosea 2:15 we can find that in this Valley of Achor (Trouble) that God could turn trouble into joy and despair into hope. Hosea 2:14-16 (AMPC): "Therefore, behold, I will allure her [Israel] and bring her into the wilderness, and I will speak tenderly and to her heart. There I will give her her vineyards and make the Valley of Achor [troubling] to be for her a door of hope and expectation. And she shall sing there and respond as in the days of her youth and as at the time when she came up out of the land of Egypt."

Our Valley of Achor will be a place of worship, a place where our trouble will be turned into hope - a place of expectation, joy, and rest...

The Valley of Decision

Good Morning... Today we have another valley to consider - the Valley of Decision. This came when I awoke this morning and heard, "It's time to make your mind up."

Too often we live with indecision. The devil loves our indecision, because he can put thoughts in our mind and play with our emotions. It creates what James talks about in James 1:8, double mindedness, a "condition" which affects our entire life. Here is how the NKJV describes it, "a double-minded man" is "unstable in all his ways." I am learning to ask the Father to help me see and perceive and have the courage to hear the answers and then to do what I am being shown to do.

In Joel 3:14 it says multitudes are in this valley. In other words, we are not alone. What decision or decisions have we been avoiding due to a crippling sense of fear? I have discovered that more often than not, the fear I'm facing I create myself through my own mental gymnastics.

Paul tells us that each of us has to make up our own mind. One person might make one decision and another person makes a different one, but what others do is not necessarily what we should do. We see this in Romans 14:5: "One person esteems one day above another; another esteems every day alike. Let each be fully convinced (persuaded) in his own mind."

Jesus said in John 14:6 that the Holy Spirit would teach and lead us. Why is it that we make decisions on our own and then ask God to bless them? Wouldn't it be better to ask the Holy Spirit ahead of time? I can't help but feel as I'm writing this that many of you are in the Valley of Decision.

It's because the Father loves us that He'll show us what to do. Please hear that! John 5:20 (NKJV): "For the Father loves the Son, and shows Him all things that He Himself does; and He will show Him greater works than these, that you may marvel."

Welcome to the Valley of Decision...

Passing Through the Valley of Baca

When the children of Israel needed to go to Jerusalem (to keep the feast days) they would often pass through the Valley of Baca, which in the Hebrew means the Valley of Weeping or the Valley of Tears.

The purpose of going to Jerusalem was to make the journey to meet with God during the biblical feasts. We are doing the same thing - journeying with a great desire to meet and draw closer to the Lord. And yes, in our journey we too will pass through the Valley of Weeping.

Yet we often find that there is provision in this valley. Psalm 84:6 (TLB) says, "When they walk through the Valley of Weeping, it will become a place of springs where pools of blessing and refreshment collect after rains!"

The psalmist tells us that God will provide.

This can only be understood when we realize that the Valley of Baca is a very dry and arid desert. History records that if God's children came into this valley and were willing to dig shallow wells, God would supernaturally fill those wells with water. This water then refreshed, restored, and strengthened them to continue the journey.

Even in the Valley of Weeping and Tears if we're willing to dig a well, God will come and fill it so we may be refreshed before continuing the journey. Often, if we're honest, though, it's easier to complain and feel sorry for ourselves.

Even in this place of our emotions feeling upside down, I know that if I am willing to dig, God will fill me up...

Yes, there are pools of blessings and refreshment in the Valley of Weeping...

The Valley of Vision

This morning as I was studying and musing with the Lord, I ended up in Isaiah chapter 22 where Isaiah speaks about the Valley of Vision. I quickly remembered Genesis 22 where God tells Abraham to take his son and go to Mount Moriah. One of the Hebrew definitions for Mount Moriah is "the land of vision."

I have often thought that in order to gain vision I needed to be on top of a mountain or at a similar vantage point which allowed me to look down from heaven. While this is true, what I didn't understand at the time is that I can get vision even in the valley.

We can indeed get vision when we're experiencing the height of the mountain but even in the low, valley times, Abba has vision for us. Imagine all these years longing for a mountaintop in order to gain vision when all along there was vision for me in the valley?!

The truth is that wherever you are today there is VISION for you. Before I ended up in Isaiah 22 I had this overwhelming burden for people who are in a valley needing to hear from God, wanting desperately to get out of that place yet not knowing that there is understanding, clarity, and vision right where they are.

Whether you are on the mountain or in the valley - there is VISION FOR YOU.

Vindication

Have you ever been wronged? Have you ever been falsely accused of something that you never did? Has someone spread lies and rumors about you? What was your response when people came to you, and having already heard the lie, had made their minds up that you were guilty?

At this point a scream is tempting. At the top of your lungs you may yell, "I didn't do it. I'm not guilty." We might even want to label the person who told them a liar.

While there are times we need to defend ourselves, there are others when we are to remain quiet. In Psalm 68:5 it says, "God is a defender." Then in Acts 8:32 when Phillip is talking to the eunuch about the scripture he is reading in Isaiah 53:7, it says about Jesus, "Now this was the passage of Scripture which he was reading 'Like a sheep He was led to the slaughter; And as a lamb before its shearer is silent, So He does not open His mouth.' " When he was being falsely accused before Pilate, it says in Matthew 26:63 that "Jesus kept silent."

Yes, there are times when we need time to defend ourselves and when we do, to act with great wisdom, asking the Holy Spirit to show us what and when to speak. A common danger is responding in our flesh and ending up being very carnal. Jesus addresses this in John 6:63: "It is the Spirit who gives life; the flesh is no help at all."

When we react in our flesh people can't hear what we're really trying to say because all they can hear is our flesh. When a person is angry, harsh, bitter, resentful, etcetera, and they're communicating a truth, it's often very hard to hear them because we can't get beyond their attitude and tone of voice. We can likely think of several examples of this - people in our lives who were undeniably right but who we didn't hear because of their negative words and attitude.

Perhaps the most powerful way we can respond to being wronged, lied about, and falsely accused is to walk in Psalm 17:2 (TLV) which says, "From Your presence comes my vindication."

Imagine this for a moment: from God's very presence comes my VINDICATION...

On one occasion I had the opportunity to live this out. A situation arose where God told me clearly not to vindicate myself, that vindication would come from "His presence." And it did. I never spoke one word in my defense. After all, we are told He is our advocate. 1 John 2:1 (NKJV): "we have an advocate with the Father, Jesus Christ the righteous."

Notice it says "We have...(present tense)...

You Have an Inheritance

Ephesians 1:11 (ESV) says, "In him we have obtained an inheritance, having been predestined according to the purpose of him who works all things according to the counsel of his will."

Imagine for a moment that you received a phone call from an attorney, and the attorney tells you that someone has died and left you an inheritance. He goes on to ask if you'd be interested in receiving it.

The amazing thing about an inheritance is that the person receiving it doesn't do anything to earn it. The inheritance is given simply because there's a relationship between that person and the person who died.

This is indeed the case with us and Jesus. It was through the death of Jesus that he obtained for us eternal life. Eternal life can't be earned by being a good person, doing good works, or following theological rules and regulations. There is nothing any of us can do that would qualify us for eternity. If being good, religious, or simply doing good works would qualify us, then Jesus' dying for mankind would have made him a fool.

As much as there is a future inheritance, Jesus left us an inheritance for now. That inheritance is entrance into and living in the Kingdom of God. Paul defines our inheritance in Romans 14:17(NKJV) "for the kingdom of God is not eating and drinking, but righteousness and peace and joy in the Holy Spirit."

Our inheritance is righteousness (right standing with God), peace, and joy – right NOW.

Determine not to let this inheritance be stolen from you... For example, if someone is angry with you, determine that you're not going to allow their anger to steal your peace and joy. If you're feeling falsely accused of something, determine not to react or respond in your flesh. Stop and think about how you like someone acting carnally toward you. Three times in the bible it says, "he held his peace."

Peace is your inheritance. Don't let people or circumstances steal it.

Position Yourself

When Jehoshaphat found himself surrounded by several armies of Syria, it was clear that unless God intervened, Jehoshaphat and all of Judah would be defeated.

As everyone gathered for prayer, God sent a prophet with the answer. In 2 chronicles 20:14-15 it says, "Then the Spirit of the Lord came upon Jahaziel the son of Zechariah, the son of Benaiah, the son of Jeiel, the son of Mattaniah, a Levite of the sons of Asaph, in the midst of the assembly. And he said, 'LISTEN all you of Judah and you inhabitants of Jerusalem, and you, King Jehoshaphat! Thus says the Lord to you: "Do not be afraid nor dismayed because of this great multitude, for the battle is not yours, but God's." "

Then Jahaziel continues to prophesy in verse 17 and says, "You will not need to fight in this battle. Position yourselves, stand still and see the salvation of the Lord, who is with you."

How were they to position themselves? The answer - 2 Chronicles 20:20-22. They were to send the worship team before the warriors. And what happened the moment they began to worship? God supernaturally defeated all the Syrian armies.

If we could only embrace and live out the simple advice to be unafraid and not worry about what we're facing, how transforming that could be! After all, it's not our battle but our Father's.

Furthermore, can it be that when we worship, God defeats our enemies?!

As we face circumstances and battles in our lives, we must seek the Lord as Jehoshaphat did to see how He will direct/position us. There is a divine strategy for every battle we will face. We find a perfect example in 2 Kings 6:8-10 (NKJV): "Now the king of Syria was making war against Israel; and he consulted with his servants, saying, 'My camp will be in such and such a place.' And the man of God sent to the king of Israel, saying, 'Beware that you do not pass this place, for the Syrians are coming down there.' Then the king of Israel sent someone to the place the man of God had told him. Thus he warned him, and he was watchful there, and not just once."

God revealed how to defeat the enemy, and they positioned the troops accordingly. Yes, hearing and doing…

When Nehemiah was rebuilding the wall surrounding Jerusalem, he "positioned" men on the wall: Nehemiah 4:13 (NKJV): "Therefore I positioned men behind the lower parts of the wall, at the openings; and I set the people according to their families, with their swords, their spears, and their bows."

There are countless times in our lives when like Jehoshaphat, we don't know what to do. Second Chronicles 20:12 (NKJV) says, "For we have no power against this great multitude that is coming against us; nor do we know what to do, but our eyes are upon You."

There is a divine strategy. Find out what it is and then POSITION yourself... After... watch what God will do.

When You Hope in Hope

While writing this I have been fighting back tears. I am feeling overwhelmed with hopelessness, yet deep inside of me there's a voice yelling, "Have hope in hope." Now the crazy thing is that while I am personally not in this place, I know that there are a number of people today who are.

When you love someone their burden becomes your burden. Because we're members of the same body (of Christ), we're connected, and when another hurts, we can hurt.

Galatians 6:2 (NKJV): "Bear one another's burdens, and so fulfill the law of Christ."

1 Corinthians 12: 25-26 (NKJV): "that there should be no schism in the body, but that the members should have the same care for one another. And if one member suffers, all the members suffer with it; or if one member is honored, all the members rejoice with it."

I am reminded of the story of Abraham, to whom God gave a prophetic promise that he would have a son. He waited and waited and waited. Then after ten years Abraham and Sarah got tired of waiting and had an idea to fulfill the prophetic promise on their own, through another woman. Her name was Hagar. Because Abraham and Sarah believed that time was running out for Sarah to have the child (she was old and beyond typical childbearing years), they "helped" God by taking matters into their own hands.

How many of us get tired of waiting and make certain decisions to help expedite God's prophetic word? Praise God that in these cases He's bigger than our mistakes and sins. Unfortunately though, as in this case, there are consequences for our poor decisions.

Hear me: GOD HAS NOT FORGOTTEN HIS PROMISE TO YOU. In Genesis 17 God appears to Abraham years after Ismael is born (perhaps twelve years later) and reminds him of the original promise. Abraham laughs inside himself while Sarah laughs out loud. Can we relate?

Now we can see the time frame that Romans 4:18 speaks about. God had renewed His promise (God hadn't changed his mind), and Romans 4:18 speaks to Abraham's response to that rekindling. Romans 4:18 (Modern English Version): "Against all hope, he (Abraham) believed in hope, that he might become the father of many nations according to what was spoken, 'So shall your descendants be.' "

Abraham hoped in hope... I am hearing this to say to you, HOPE IN HOPE... Yes, He is FAITHFUL WHO PROMISED, even when we are not. Hold on to what He has promised...

Go ahead; hope in hope...

You Will Not Spend Eternity in Heaven

I remember being in the Dominican Republic in July of 2107 and doing a leaders' conference for pastors. I told them that I was about to share something that would shock them.

I then asked how many of them were expecting to spend eternity in heaven. Everyone raised their hands. I told them that this would not happen. Then...there was a gasp of air that filled the room. They looked at me in shock and disbelief as if they had invited me to come only to find that I taught heresy.

I told them that while it's true that we'll go to heaven, heaven is not our final destination. Because we've believed we'll be in heaven forever, we never viewed this life we're living now as a time to prepare for our future. I had them turn to Genesis 1:26-28 (NKJV) and I read, "Then God said, 'Let us make man in our image, according to our likeness; let them have dominion over the fish of the sea, over the birds of the air, and over the cattle, over all the earth and over every creeping thing that creeps on the earth.' So God created man in His own image; in the image of God He created him; male and female He created them. Then God blessed them, and God said to them, 'Be fruitful and multiply; fill the earth and subdue it; have dominion over the fish of the sea, over the birds of the air, and over every living thing that moves on the earth.' "

We then talked about the picture God had portrayed, a picture showing what we were created to do -- to rule, reign, and govern. God's original intent and purpose was exactly that. It was His purpose from the beginning, and He hasn't changed His mind.

I then had them turn to Revelation 5:10 (NKJV): "...and have made us kings and priests to our God; And we shall reign on the earth." We are to rule, reign, and govern where? We then turned to Revelation 21:1-2 which tells us that God's Kingdom is coming to earth. Verses 1-2 (NKJV): "Now I saw a new heaven and a new earth, for the first heaven and the first earth had passed away."

With this understanding the parable of the talents in Matthew 25 makes more sense. Reading verse 21: "His lord said to him, 'Well done, good and faithful servant; you were faithful over a few things, I will make you ruler over many things. Enter into the joy of your lord.' " The faithfulness of using the gifts God has given us will qualify us to rule, reign, and govern in God's Kingdom on earth.

So no, you were not created to spend eternity in heaven. Perhaps that will give you a different perspective of how to live on earth.

Weapons of Our Warfare

I continue to discover that the Bible says what it says, and there's no need to look for deeper revelation.

A movie came out years ago called "Mortal Combat." Its theme was good versus evil. When we awake each day that same war is all around us. Satan would like nothing better than to unleash upon us circumstances and demonic forces which would cause us to fall, fail, and live lives of discouragement, depression, and hopelessness all the while stealing from us who we really are.

It's time we stood our ground. Its time to stop allowing Satan to steal from us and our family. It's time we take back what the enemy has stolen. Read Ezra 6.

I am mystified about how when we're engaged in a spiritual battle we try and use natural methodology to fight. Literally, when all hell breaks loose, we rely on natural methods. For example, using anger as our weapon. In reality the anger we are displaying more often than not is just a fleshly response to a spiritual situation, stripping God of the opportunity to work on our behalf.

Second Corinthians 10:3-4 (The Passion Translation) says, "For although we live in the natural realm, we don't wage a military campaign employing human weapons, using manipulation to achieve our aims. Instead, our spiritual weapons are energized with divine power."

Spiritual weapons are things like prayer, fasting, worshipping, and living a consistent biblical life style. Using carnal weapons, on the other hand, becomes like throwing gasoline on a fire.

One of our greatest weapons are prophetic words God has spoken to us. In 1 Timothy 1:18 (NKJV) it says, "This charge I commit to you, son Timothy, according to the prophecies previously made concerning you, that by them you may wage the good warfare." Use God's word (the bible) and what He has prophesied to us as weapons. They are powerful.

Even though we have many thoughts and feelings which don't align, fight! There are numerous scriptures declaring who we are: sons and daughters, ambassadors, precious, special treasures, called, chosen, adopted, anointed, sanctified, redeemed, appointed, kings, and priests. Say them out loud, say loudly to Satan, "This is what my Father says to me, and you're a liar. I will not listen to your lies or deception."

Declare what your Father has told you- then announce/declare/shout the prophetic word you've been given. Trade in your carnal weapons for supernatural ones.

Expectation

Did you wake up today expecting to encounter God? Or expecting that the Holy Spirit was going to teach you something? Is He going to show you something, going to lead you? Do you have a sense that today won't be like any other ordinary day?

Even though we believe He is omnipresent, most of us have little or no expectation that on any given day something supernatural will occur. God is always present, but seemingly, nothing big usually happens. Why is that?

I often get a picture in my mind of deep ruts created by walking on the same path over, over, and over again. Those ruts have a name. They're called routine or habitual living.

There is a story in the books of Acts about a lame man with an expectation. As you read this you'll see that his confidence was in money and what someone else could do for him. Is that us? Are we thinking that if only we have more money then such and such could happen? Or if this person would do this for me, then this other thing could happen?

Here's the story: Acts 3:1-5 (The Message Bible): "One day at three o'clock in the afternoon, Peter and John were on their way into the Temple for prayer meeting. At the same time there was a man crippled from birth being carried up. Every day he was set down at the Temple gate, the one named Beautiful, to beg from those going into the Temple. When he saw Peter and John about to enter the Temple, he asked for a handout. Peter, with John at his side, looked him straight in the eye and said, 'Look here.' He looked up, expecting to get something from them."

Every time I read this story I can hear God say, "Put away your tin cup." It's easy to fall into trading our identities as sons or daughters and seeing ourselves as beggars. We can actually have a beggar's mentality, placing our expectation in carnal, rather than spiritual things.

Your life – if you let it - will be filled with such incredible joy and excitement. You'll wake up in the morning wondering what God is going to do… Perhaps another word for expectation is FAITH.

For the lame man it was just another ordinary day. Today can be ordinary, or.. it can be extraordinary.

A natural day or a supernatural day - which will it be for you?!

Why Not You?

Why is it that we can look at others and see their potential but can't see our own?

Beyond this, people actually want to be someone else. Instead of celebrating who they are, they daydream about having another identity, always believing that God will use someone else instead of them.

This has to end. People are being robbed - robbed from entering into the plans God has for them. Their identity is being stolen, and they're being deceived and lied to. As long as this continues people won't reach their divine destiny.

In 2 Corinthians 10:12 we see Paul cautioning us not to compare ourselves to others. Continuing to belittle ourselves causes an attitude of unworthiness, a mindset that causes people to shrink back and to develop an expectation that God will use someone else.

We fall into an attitude of looking at who we aren't instead of who we are. Listen to the word God spoke to Isaiah about Israel. Isaiah 43:1 (NKJV): "But now, thus says the Lord, who created you, O Jacob, And He who formed you, O Israel: 'Fear not, for I have redeemed you; I have called you by your name; You are Mine.' "

You're God's amazing and unique child.

Which one of you who has children doesn't see the great value and potential in each one?

If we wait to be perfect we lose sight that in Christ we are seen as complete. The only perfect person who lived was Jesus. Paul writes in Colossians 2:10 (NKJV): "...and you are complete in Him." Our father works through imperfect people.

God wants to use you... Why not you? Why not now?

The Haggai Principle

Being a pastor for over four decades, I have spent countless hours counseling people, and in the process, have learned a big lesson about expectations.

As much as I wanted to give people input which would change their lives, too often nothing would happen. We would meet week after week, and week after week nothing changed. I would try this and try that. I would give them scriptures one week and different scriptures the next week. I would faithfully pray for all of them. And when I'd ask them if they had reviewed the verses, more often than not they said they had never looked at them. When I asked them if they had prayed about the things we were sharing, again, more often than not they said they hadn't prayed at all or had prayed very little.

What became clear was that I was working at it more than they were. Week after week this happened. It only took me about 30 of the 40 years to see this.

Revelation came through Haggai 1:6 (AMPC): "He who earns wages has earned them to put them in a bag with holes in it." The Holy Spirit showed me that I had been investing in people who were acting in like matter. And similar to putting water into a sieve, everything was emptying out in the most fruitless way.

After realizing this I addressed it right away with the people I counseled. I told them that I would invest in them, but if I worked harder at it than they did, we would stop meeting.

Though I have applied the Haggai principle to counseling, it also holds true in many other areas of our lives. For example, a pastor may pour his life into people for the sake of building leaders, but as much as he invests, they don't appreciate it, are unreliable, undependable, and say yes but don't really follow through. They're with you in attitude one week but not the next. Behind your back they criticize your leadership, but in reality, do very little to help you lead.

Yes, investing in people is critical, but so is having a realistic expectation of return in that investment.

Lessons from Gold Miners

The first miner:

These were the miners who worked the mines day after day. They would spend long hours using crude picks to pierce the solid rock of the caves they called mines. These miners worked their mines day after day and year after year with no success, and many of them gave up. They would abandon their mines and with that, their dreams. Once a mine was abandoned, it could be claimed by another who immediately went to work mining it.

It has been recorded that there were occasions when the new miners began to work their mines, and the very first pick into the rock hit gold.

The lesson here? Don't allow discouragement and disappointment to cause you to abandon your dreams. Listen to the word of the Lord from Habakkuk 2:3 (NKJV): "For the vision is yet for an appointed time; But at the end it will speak, and it will not lie. Though it tarries, wait for it; Because it will surely come, It will not tarry." IT WILL COME… I waited 22 and 25 years for the fulfillment of two prophetic promises.

The second miner: (Unfortunately, I can relate to this miner more than I'd like to admit.)

This person works the rivers and streams panning for gold. Day after day they pan looking for gold. On the odd occasion they find a nugget, but sadly many of these miners never appreciate or value the small nugget. Dissatisfied and ungrateful, they say to themselves, "It's only a small nugget."

Many of them cash in the nugget and misspend the money because they never assign true value to it. They're looking instead for a big nugget. Because of this, these miners live in frustration and disappointment and are ungrateful for what they've found.

The lesson is pretty clear. We must truly value every nugget we find, however small. Instead of looking for the big nugget, we should value the small nugget and then the next one and the one after that. For too many years I failed to cherish and honor every nugget the Lord gave me. The small nugget wasn't big enough, but what I didn't know was that if I saved and valued each nugget, I would soon have a jar of nuggets which together had great value.

Because of my dissatisfaction and ungratefulness, my life was diminished. Thankfully I have since learned to never devalue anything the Lord gives me, whether big or small. Otherwise I become like the small child who is ungrateful for everything, no matter the sacrifice to bring it.

Embracing Philippians 4:4 (NKJV) has been pivotal: "Rejoice in the Lord always. Again, I will say, rejoice."

Ricochet Rabbit

So who is Ricochet Rabbit?

Years ago there was a cartoon that took place in the Wild West. Ricochet Rabbit was a character in the story who worked as a sheriff in the town of Hoop 'n' Holler. Ricochet would bounce off stationary objects yelling, "Bing-bing-bing!"

Ricochet Rabbit reminds me of us sometimes - we are often all over the place.

This gets played out with the gifts God has given us, not wanting what we do have and desiring things we don't. For example, while I can teach the Word of God, I am not a teacher. In the early 2000s though, I started hearing that I should be more of a teacher and do less prophetic ministry, so I began to go in this direction.

What a disaster. I wasn't happy, and the congregation wasn't happy because of two things: my anointing wasn't that of a teacher but of someone who was apostolic/prophetic, and related to this, I was trying to be somebody God never intended me to be.

Paul speaks to this in 1 Timothy 4:14-15 (NKJV): "Do not neglect the gift that is in you, which was given to you by prophecy with the laying on of the hands of the eldership. Meditate on these things; give yourself entirely to them, that your progress may be evident to all."

The point is to not overlook the gift that you have. Meditate (consider, muse, ponder) on the gift and how it operates in you. There is a tendency people have to try and copy or mimic how the gift they have operates in someone else. Hear me - BE YOU- YOU'RE AN ORIGINAL. You were never called to be someone else. In fact, rejoice in who you are, not in who you're not.

Paul says, give yourself to the gift you have, not the gift you don't have. When we do this it becomes very evident to everyone around what gift we have, which in turn encourages others to be who they are as well. If your gift is hospitality, then give yourself to hospitality; if it's listening, then listen.

Just be you and be grateful for it. As Paul writes in 1 Corinthians 15:10 (NKJV): "But by the grace of God I am what I am" and then in

Romans 12:5-7 (NKJV) "So we, being many, are one body in Christ, and individually members of one another. Having then gifts differing according to the grace that is given to us, let us use them: if prophecy, let us prophesy in proportion to our faith; or ministry, let us use it in our ministering; he who teaches, in teaching."

Be who you are; use what you have...

I Don't Want to Go

Perhaps by now you've discovered that as much as we try and control our lives, when it comes right down to it, we simply can't.

At the same time, you might have discovered that God has different ways to work things both in and out of us. And many of those methods we would've never chosen. In fact, there was a time in my life when I told the Lord "to go pick on somebody else."

At the time it seemed that God was picking on me yet not working on others. I can just see God laughing. Yet I can tell you that after some of the work was done I just raised my hands in worship and thanked Him for what He'd done in spite of me. I also better understood Philippians 2:13 (NIV): "for it is God who works in you to will and to act in order to fulfill his good purpose." God was actually molding me more into His likeness. In fact, He was definitely answering some of my prayers - I just wasn't fond of some of His methods!

I can so relate to what Jesus said to Peter in John 21:8 (NKJV): "Most assuredly, I say to you, when you were younger, you girded yourself and walked where you wished; but when you are old, you will stretch out your hands, and another will gird you and carry you where you do not wish." Yes, God takes us places we don't want to go.

These periods in our lives often coincide with trials that we think are beyond what we can bear/handle. There have been times when I said to the Lord, "Okay, I can't take any more," and lo and behold, very often things got worse. But here is a promise you can hold onto in 1 Corinthians 10:13 (NTE): "Every test that comes upon you is normal for human beings. But God is faithful: he won't let you be tested beyond your ability. Along with the testing, he will provide the way of escape, so that you can bear it."

Know this: GOD WILL PROVIDE A WAY OUT for every trial you will ever experience.

Oh, I have a PS: it might take some time.

Teaching Yourself - That's Silly

It was somewhere in the middle of the 1970s that I was studying for the ministry. I would go to the kitchen table with commentaries - Greek and Hebrew Lexicons - and would study for hours. I began to struggle because I was reading excerpts from commentaries that were in conflict with what my heart and Spirit were saying to me.

This went on for months.

Finally, one day the Lord asked me, "Are you tired yet?" I knew exactly what He was talking about. He then elaborated, "Are you tired of teaching yourself"? He then told me that I was silly. With that comment I knew that what would follow would be something profound. He went on to ask me why was I believing what theologians had written considering that so many of them were not even believers. He also wondered why I was teaching myself when He had sent the Holy Spirit to teach me. With that I remembered John 14:26 (NKJV): "But the

Helper, the Holy Spirit, whom the Father will send in My name, He will teach you all things."

Since that day when I go to read or study, I do something pretty wise -- I ask the Holy Spirit to teach me.

And do you know what happens? He does...

The Call to Go Deeper

There are multiple seasons in our lives. One is where we're stuck and often don't recognize it. We're working hard at trying to receive from the Lord but to no avail.

The story in Luke chapter five has some answers for us.

Peter and the rest of his crew had fished all night and hadn't caught anything. Jesus sees Peter washing his nets and asks him to moor his boat so Jesus can preach from it, as the crowd has become too large.

Now we can look at Luke 5:4-7 (NKJV): "When He had stopped speaking, He said to Simon, 'Launch out into the deep and let down your nets for a catch.' But Simon answered and said to Him, 'Master, we have toiled all night and caught nothing; nevertheless at Your word I will let down the net.' And when they had done this, they caught a great number of fish, and their net was breaking. So they signaled to their partners in the other boat to come and help them. And they came and filled both the boats, so that they began to sink."

So what can we glean from this? First, we see Peter washing his nets after catching nothing all night. Why didn't they catch anything? Perhaps they were fishing in the wrong location. It's like us when we're trying to reap a spiritual harvest but may be fishing in waters which are too shallow. Remember verse four, where Jesus advises Peter to launch out into the deep.

Peter responds and launches out deeper. The choice we are facing is the one he faced: Shall we stay in shallow waters or do what we see Peter do? "Master, we have toiled all night and caught nothing; nevertheless at Your word I will let down the net."

There are seasons when we're in Peter's place: we have become too comfortable, settling into ruts and routines. It's as if we've been swimming in the shallow end of the pool and now the Holy Spirit is calling us into the deep.

Can you hear that the Holy Spirit is calling you to GO DEEPER?

By responding to go deeper, our boats, like Peter's, may just overflow.

When you go deeper, expect that the harvest will be great.

Keep Your Accounts Short

This is another "down under" expression that Pastor Glenn would often say.

It means that as soon as we recognize sin in our lives, we need to deal with it. Not doing so leads us to discover that we have a rather lengthy list in our lives.

Thus, the admonition: keep your accounts short.

I don't know why the idea of repentance has become almost like condemnation. Many Christians today have a difficult time repenting when repenting means to have a change of mind and to go in the opposite direction, making a 180-degree turn from where we are.

The following verse from Acts three may encourage all of us to keep our accounts short. Acts 3:19 (AMP): "So repent [change your inner self—your old way of thinking, regret past sins] and return [to God—seek His purpose for your life], so that your sins may be wiped away [blotted out, completely erased], so that times of refreshing may come from the presence of the Lord [restoring you like a cool wind on a hot day]."

I could sense a cool wind blowing as I wrote this.

So go ahead, change your mind. Can you see the blackboard in front of you? On it are the things you need to repent of, and the moment you begin I can see the black board being erased. Then the Lord hands you a piece of chalk and says, "Go ahead and write your tomorrow." The air in the room smells like the air outside after a warm, spring rain - everything clean and crisp.

Take a deep breath because God wants to refresh you and surround you with His presence...

Indeed... keep your accounts short.

Step Forward

In three of the gospels we find a man in a synagogue with a withered hand.

I liken that to crippled people attending church. Their crippling can be physical, mental, and/or emotional. When a person is in this state it's hard for them to do anything. Even to take just one small step forward seems impossible.

Here is Mark's account of that story: Mark 3:1-3 (NKJV): "And He entered the synagogue again, and a man was there who had a withered hand. So they watched Him closely, whether He would heal him on the Sabbath, so that they might accuse Him. And He said to the man who had the withered hand, 'Step forward.' " and then in verse five: " 'Stretch out your hand.' And he stretched it out, and his hand was restored."

You can see that what Jesus asked the crippled man to do was to step forward.

It's possible that in all of our lives where we're crippled, the Holy Spirit is instructing us to initiate faith by taking a step. It's possible that the man with the withered hand wouldn't have gotten healed if he hadn't taken that ONE STEP.

Jesus didn't ask him to run a marathon. He just requested that he take one step.

Yes, there are times when Jesus comes to us and asks us to STEP FORWARD...

Tomorrow

I can hear Annie (the red headed girl in the musical) clearing her throat as she prepares to once again sing the song "Tomorrow." To be honest I think it's the theme song for many Christians' lives.

It describes the deadly disease of procrastination. I call it deadly because it has killed many dreams. Killed hope and joy... Tomorrow I'll change. Tomorrow I'll become involved. Tomorrow I'll become obedient to tithe. Tomorrow I'll apologize, tell them I'm sorry. Ya, tomorrow, then the next day and the next, all the while feeling inside ourselves a sense of incompletion or even grieving.

Sometimes it's the Holy Spirit inside of us who's grieving. We can actually grieve the Holy Spirit. Ephesians 4:30 (NKJV) admonishes us: "And do not grieve the Holy Spirit of God, by whom you were sealed for the day of redemption." Haven't there been days when you're irritable, cranky, discontented, unsettled, and bewildered and you know something's not right but don't know what it is? This can be an indicator that we're grieving the Holy Spirit.

What can cause our procrastination? Several things, but one is that we may lack confidence that God will work through us. We're focusing on our weaknesses rather than God's enabling power. We are affected by our fear, failures, shortcomings, and sin. It's the perpetual lie YOU'RE NOT - NOT THIS, NOT THAT, and so on.

And sometimes, sometimes we're just plain lazy.

But there's a solution to our tomorrow attitude. It's in Judges 6:14 (NKJV) when God is speaking to Gideon to deliver Israel from the Midianites: "Then the Lord turned to him and said, 'Go in this might of yours, and you shall save Israel from the hand of the Midianites. Have I not sent you?' "

Whatever God asks us to do we don't do alone. He is ever-present to empower us to succeed in whatever He shows us to do. We need to remember 2 Corinthians 4:7 (NKJV): "But we have this treasure in earthen vessels, that the excellence of the power may be of God and not of us."

Join me in replacing the song "Tomorrow" with "This is the Day."

The Courtroom

I want you to picture a courtroom.

There in the courtroom you'll see the judge (the Father), the prosecuting attorney/your adversary (Greek meaning one who is legally against you - see 1 Peter 5:8). This is Satan.

We read in the book of Revelation that Satan brings accusations of our guilt before the throne of God day and night. Revelation 12:10 (NKJV): "Then I heard a loud voice saying in heaven, 'Now salvation, and strength, and the kingdom of our God, and the power of His Christ have come, for the accuser of our brethren, who accused them before our God day and night, has been cast down.' "

Then in this courtroom sitting opposite the "accuser" is your defense attorney, your advocate (Greek meaning one who is legally for you) - Jesus. First John 2:1 (NKJV): "My little children, these things I write to you, so that you may not sin. And if anyone sins, we have an Advocate with the Father, Jesus Christ the righteous." Sitting next to Jesus is you, the accused.

The trial begins with the adversary (Satan) standing up and telling the judge (the Father) that we are guilty of breaking the law. Just as he finishes, our advocate (Jesus) stands up and tells the judge/Father that he personally paid for your sin/crime. The Judge grabs the gavel and makes an incredibly loud sound that fills the courtroom as the gavel hits the judge's bench.

The Judge then stands up and points to you declaring, "NOT GUILTY!" There is a thunderous applause as all the angels begin rejoicing and singing "NOT GUILTY." The proceedings continue with

Satan accusing, Jesus defending, and the judge declaring "Not Guilty." The angels rejoice, and you fall on your face and weep.

This goes on for hours until finally the judge stands up and throws Satan out of the courtroom as the gavel comes down and hits the podium. He holds up a legal document which reads simply - NOT GUILTY.

YOU ARE NOT GUILTY…

Stir Up

Are you waiting for God to increase your anointing? Are you waiting for Him to do something? Perhaps the reality is that God is waiting for YOU.

This is reminiscent of the person who wants to lose weight, but instead of exercising and watching their diet, they pray. The person who wants a new car but never saves money or gets a second job. They just pray and ask God for one. I am not saying that God can't supernaturally help us lose weight or provide a new car, but very often what He wants to do is to enable us to exercise, diet, save money, get a second job, etcetera.

Some want to teach the word of God but they never study. Others want to prophesy but don't read the scriptures about ministering prophetically, nor do they spend much time in prayer or worship. Some want to develop the gift of hospitality but never invite people over. People may want to serve but never volunteer. Others want a fire but never gather wood. It's easy to see that with every gift there are at least a few things that we have the responsibility to actually DO.

Paul writes Timothy to remind him not to neglect the gift of God that is in him. This neglect is possible for any one of us. We can have a gift but can overlook it by being preoccupied with other things or feeling insecure and unconfident and thus fail to use what God has supernaturally put in us.

It's interesting that some fifteen years later Paul needs to write Timothy again to give him some practical advice and counsel. Second Timothy 1:6 (NKJV) says, "Therefore I remind you to stir up the gift of God which is in you through the laying on of my hands." The Greek word rendered "stir up" literally means to kindle up, to fan into flame; anazopureo, used of the resuscitation of a flame. John Gill's Commentary says, "The word used is a metaphor reminiscent of coals from a fire which having been covered with ashes, are "almost extinct, and need to be blown up into a flame."

So my question is... what are you doing with your gift? Whatever you do, don't neglect it... Stir it up, because you are needed!

Are You Uncomfortable?

There are times that God wants us to grow, to move on from where we are. We all enjoy being comfortable, yet there are times when we can get too much so.

It's like having an old pair of shoes that we love but are no longer viable. They offer no support for our feet and beyond that will damage our feet if we persist in wearing them. One of the reasons we avoid new ones is that the breaking-in process is too uncomfortable. New shoes feel awkward and yes, there's a good chance we'll even get blisters.

Yet God loves us so much and sees all that we're created to be, all the Divine Potential… So what does He do? He uses situations and circumstances to remove our comfort.

A good example is the way God designed eagles. At a certain point the mother eagle, who's been in the nest with her eaglet children, needs to teach them to fly.

What can we assume the eaglets want to do in this situation - stay in the nest, of course. It's comfortable and safe. Just like us. So what does the mother eagle do? She begins to pull the nest apart to make it uncomfortable for the eaglets to stay. The solution for the eaglet becomes to move to another part of the nest. The mother's response? She arrives and proceeds to tear apart that portion of the nest. Soon there isn't one spot in the nest for the eaglet to "hide."

We can picture the eaglet becoming increasingly uncomfortable. And if that isn't bad enough, in a very short period of time their "mama" is going to pick them up and drop them one by one from the nest. She'll then swoop down to catch each eaglet only to drop them again. Why does she do this? She wants her child to fly.

Does God do this? Most definitely. Read this interesting verse from Deuteronomy 32:11 (NKJV): "As an eagle stirs up its nest, Hovers over its young, Spreading out its wings, taking them up, Carrying them on its wings."

God will make you uncomfortable because he wants you to FLY…

You Want Me to Do What?

I really believe that we have missed many answers from God for two basic reasons.

1. We are looking for logical answers to satisfy our "natural" minds.

2. We don't have the capacity to hear unusual/peculiar answers.

Let's look at a number of examples:

Exodus 14:16: God tells Moses to part the Red Sea by lifting up his hand over it. Does that make sense? Verse 16, "But lift up your rod, and stretch out your hand over the sea and divide it. And the children of Israel shall go on dry ground through the midst of the sea."

Moses obeys God, and the Red Sea opens, allowing nearly two million people to cross over to the other side.

When the children of Israel were to cross the Jordon River, the priests who carried the ark stood in the river, and 90 miles upstream, the river was stopped. Joshua 3:8 (NKJV): "When you have come to the edge of the water of the Jordan, you shall stand in the Jordan."

The 12 priests stand in the Jordan River, and everyone crosses over.

In Judges 6 Gideon starts out with 32,000 men against the 135,000 Midianites. God tells him that he has too many men. God shrinks Gideon's army down to 300 men. Judges 7:7 (NKJV): "Then the Lord said to Gideon, 'By the three hundred men who lapped I will save you, and deliver the Midianites into your hand. Let all the other people go, every man to his place.' "

Yes, with only 300 men God defeats an army of 135,000.

Jehoshaphat wants to know if he should join forces with Ahad to defeat the Syrians. God uses a prophetic word to tell Jehoshaphat to dig ditches. He doesn't say, "Go fight." He says, "Dig ditches."

As crazy as it sounds, they dig the ditches, and God fills them with water. Because the soil is red, the enemy sees all the ditches filled with what they believe is blood and so they turn around and flee.

These are but a few of the countless examples of God providing answers that DON'T MAKE SENSE... YOU WANT ME TO DO WHAT?

What About Him?

Here we are in the last book of John. Jesus has just asked Peter three times if he loves him and ends up telling Peter three times "Feed My Sheep." It had to be a hard thing for Peter to hear.

Instead of taking the time to think about what Jesus has said to him, Peter once again says something "stupid." John 21:2:1: "Peter, seeing him (meaning John), said to Jesus, 'But Lord, what about this man?' " Jesus responds in verse 22, "If I will that he remain till I come, what is that to you? You follow Me."

Why is it that when God is dealing with us we suddenly tend to become concerned with what He's doing in the lives of others? Jesus has the perfect answer... Never mind - you follow me.

Truth be told we all have a difficult enough time dealing with our own issues, so why do we even give a thought to other people's? Paul cautions the Corinthians in 2 Corinthians 10:12 not to compare themselves with others, and the same should be true for us.

The reality is that worrying about what God is doing or not doing in someone else's life only serves as a distraction.

The Wheel Within the Wheel

In Ezekiel 1:16 (NKJV) it says that there is "a wheel in the middle of a wheel." This describes so many periods of our lives when we find God doing one thing while simultaneously He is doing something else.

There is one problem or situation in our lives and at the same time there is another problem or situation. There is a certain depth to a situation and at the same time another depth still.

When there are multiple things going on at varying depths, we are in need of tremendous discernment, wisdom, and understanding. Over or undervaluing the situation or jumping to conclusions is tempting, but we need to resist because doing so is often ridiculous. Eliminating an ant with a sledge hammer or fighting a forest fire with a water pistol are two examples which come to mind.

Seeking both wisdom and understanding is key. Proverbs 4:7 (NKJV): "Wisdom is the principal thing; Therefore get wisdom. And in all your getting, get understanding." Proverbs 2:1-4 (MSG): "Good friend, take to heart what I'm telling you; collect my counsels and guard them with your life. Tune your ears to the world of Wisdom; set your heart on a life of understanding."

That's right— make insight your priority, and don't take no for an answer. You have to be diligent and search for it like a prospector panning for gold, like an adventurer on a treasure hunt.

We need to have the same anointing that the sons of Issachar had as we read 2 Chronicles 12:32 (MEV): "From the sons of Issachar, those having understanding of times and what Israel should do."

Reading the Room

What does this mean? When we walk into a room, whether it be a social event like a birthday party, or a business meeting or church service, we all have the capacity to get a sense of the environment.

When we go to a friend's birthday party, for example… On the surface everyone is chatting, laughing, and seemingly having a terrific time, but… we can sense there's more going on in that room besides the party. We sense an atmosphere of tension, frustration, and even anger. By knowing this we can know what to say and what to avoid saying, what to do, and what not to do.

Let's say you're running a meeting, and it's your responsibility to facilitate. What do you do? The answer is found in 1 Samuel 10:7(NKJV): "And let it be, when these signs come to you, that you do as the occasion demands; for God is with you."

It says for you to do something. Exactly what are you to do? You are to ask the question of the Lord: "Lord, what do you want to do at this very moment?" We are not to necessarily run the meeting like we did the last time, though we tend to try and do that. Each experience demands its own calling out for wisdom.

It's like sailing -- you have to know the strength and the direction of the wind so you can adjust your sails from light to heavier weight. You can't use the same ones for every situation.

It's one thing to discern what's happening in a room; it's quite another to be able to appropriately facilitate/manage in the moment.

You might ask, well, how can I discern what is happening in a room/meeting? In Isaiah 21:3 we read how Isaiah was able to discern.

He felt it, he heard it, and he saw it. Verse 3 (NKJV): "Therefore my loins are filled with pain; Pangs have taken hold of me, like the pangs of a woman in labor. I was distressed when I heard it; I was dismayed when I saw it."

Our Father, equip us for the job - You can read the room.

Team Ministry

For so many years the church has, in my opinion, overemphasized the role and the person of the senior pastor. I believe I am qualified to speak about this considering I was a senior pastor for 25 years, an associate pastor for 11 years, and a youth/young adult leader/pastor for many years as well.

Somewhere in the mid-1980s the leadership of the Church recognized that senior pastors were not being given the respect and honor they deserved. In effect, the senior pastor was everyone's buddy, being referred to by their first name without ever giving permission for it. The problem at least here in New England is that when people are on a first-name basis, the pastor is seen as a chum and not the Man or Woman of God that God has appointed him/her to be. It created a familiar spirit.

So in order to establish respect and honor for a senior pastor, the church has taught people to accord honor to the person in this position. Like so many adjustments though, it went too far the other way, making no room for the development of team ministry. Unlike a pendulum, which usually swings from one extreme to the other and eventually finds a resting point, the question of how to treat our senior pastor has found no good resolution.

I'll say this again: we need to honor and respect God's appointed man or woman. Yet we also have to learn to honor every person in the body of Christ and by doing so to build up the body with their various gifts. The senior pastor should be honored by all means. But we can't do it in exclusion of everyone else.

Here are a couple of scriptures to consider:

Romans 12:10 (NKJV): "Be kindly affectionate to one another with brotherly love, in honor giving preference to one another."

Romans 13:7 (NKJV): "Render therefore to all their due: taxes to whom taxes are due, customs to whom customs, fear to whom fear, honor to whom honor."

Here's my perspective: in the Old Testament God worked through individuals – priests, prophets, or kings - yet in the New Testament Jesus gives us the new model of team ministry. He sent the disciples out two by two, and as he did everything, NOT unintentionally.

Mark 6:7 (NKJV): "And He called the twelve to Himself, and began to send them out two by two, and gave them power over unclean spirits."

Luke 10:1 (NKJV): "After these things the Lord appointed seventy others also, and sent them two by two before His face into every city and place where He Himself was about to go."

By sending them out as a team, if one of them became discouraged, the other one could be the encourager. When two people agree on something the power of God is released.

Matthew 18:19 (NKJV): "Again I say to you that if two of you agree on earth concerning anything that they ask, it will be done for them by My Father in heaven."

Then we have the concept of the five-fold ministry. It's called the five-fold and not the one-fold ministry for a reason. There are five distinct gifts working together to equip, train, and bring the body of Christ to maturity. Ephesians 4:11-14 (NKJV): "And He Himself gave some to be apostles, some prophets, some evangelists, and some pastors and teachers, for the equipping of the saints for the work of ministry, for the [e]edifying of the body of Christ, till we all come to the unity of the faith and of the knowledge of the Son of God, to a perfect man, to the measure of the stature of the fullness of Christ; that we should no longer be children, tossed to and fro and carried about with every wind of doctrine, by the trickery of men, in the cunning craftiness of deceitful plotting."

I encourage everyone to find a team and work together.

Get Yourself Ready

Elisha was an old man, too old to travel. Like Elijah, he had raised up a school of prophets.

It's so important to try and raise up others to follow in our footsteps, the prayer being that one day they'll far surpass us. As in Second Kings, the day comes for the release of that training. In this account Elisha sends a young prophet to anoint Jehu king of Israel. "And Elisha the prophet called one of the sons of the prophets, and said to him, 'Get yourself ready, take this flask of oil in your hand, and go to Ramoth Gilead.' " (2 Kings 9:1)

The idea of getting ourselves ready means we must be trained and equipped to do the work of the ministry each of us is called to. As much as you can, find yourself in a position to be mentored.

Even if you do receive mentoring though, in the end it's your heart which needs to be right. You can have all the training in the world but the one thing that's always necessary is having a good spirit. You can say the right words but with a wrong heart. Be aware of this, because there was a time in my own ministry where I was functioning in ministry but my heart wasn't right.

Has a minister (or for that matter, anyone) ever talked to you when their message was right, but it was hard to hear them because of their attitude or spirit?

For years now I've been hearing the Holy Spirit say, "Get yourself ready." Notice it says, "yourself." No one can do it for you. The problem I've seen over and over again is that the person has the chance to be used, but they aren't ready. A person's lack of preparation will cause them to be held back and not released. A person going to war wouldn't send an ill-prepared person into battle, never mind have them lead.

The Holy Spirit is about to do something on the earth. ARE YOU READY?

Left Alone

After twenty years of being apart, the day had come for Jacob to reconnect with his brother Esau. Jacob wasn't sure how Esau would react to seeing him again, so Jacob divided his family. He sent one wife one way and his other wife a different way. He did this just in case Esau attacked his family. By dividing them there was a greater chance at least some would survive.

After he sends his wives on their way the Bible says in Genesis 32:24 (NKJV): "Then Jacob was left alone; and a Man wrestled with him until the breaking of day." It says, "he was left alone" to wrestle the Lord.

There are times, in fact there are lots of them, when God will orchestrate our being alone -- just us and the Lord. These are special times where there is something the Lord really wants to do in our lives. Like in the case of Jacob, after wrestling all night, God changed him so much that He gave him a new name. Jacob became Israel, which means "may God prevail." Biblically a name change always signifies a change in identity. And God really enjoys changing us into another person!

In First Samuel chapter 30 David and his men return home to Ziklag only to find that the Amalekites have raided the town, burned the city, and taken all the women and children captive. All of David's men blame David and consider stoning him. In verse six it says, "Now David was greatly distressed, for the people spoke of stoning him, because the soul of all the people was grieved, every man for his sons and his daughters. But David strengthened himself in the Lord his God."

David is alone, discouraged, and heartbroken. When you're alone and broken and everyone is against you, what do you do? You strengthen (encourage) yourself.

Some of God's greatest work is done when we're alone...

Prophetic Words

The gift of prophecy is often not allowed to operate in the church because it can cause too many problems. Sadly, it's not taught correctly in many churches, mistakes are made and often not corrected, and extremes are unfortunately permitted – all these to bad effect.

When we actually follow the clear scriptures on prophesying, however, the results are amazing. 1 Corinthians 14:25 (NKJV) describes it this way: "And thus the secrets of his heart are revealed; and so, falling down on his face, he will worship God and report that God is truly among you." When prophecy and prophetic ministry are done correctly they cause people to have greater intimacy with the Lord, and the result is to fall "down on their face" in worship.

Thankfully the Bible gives us clarity as to the nature and benefit of prophecy and also instruction on how it should be carried out in the church (though it has its place outside of the church as well). Let's look at what the Bible says. These are just a few verses:

1 Corinthians 14:1 (NKJV): "Pursue love, and desire spiritual gifts, but especially that you may prophesy."

1 Corinthians 14:3 (NKJV): "But he who prophesies speaks edification and exhortation and comfort to men." (- the core value of prophesying)

1 Corinthians 14:29-33 (MEV): "Let two or three prophets speak, and let the others judge. If anything is revealed to another that sits by, let the first keep silent. For you may all prophesy one by one, that all may learn and all may be encouraged. The spirits of the prophets are

subject to the prophets. For God is not the author of confusion, but of peace, as in all churches of the saints."

1 Corinthians 14:39 (NKJV): "Therefore, brethren, desire earnestly to prophesy, and do not forbid to speak with tongues."

1 Thessalonians 5 :20-21 (NKJV) : "Do not despise prophecies. Test all things; hold fast what is good." The Amplified Bible says, "Do not scorn or reject gifts of prophecy or prophecies [spoken revelations— words of instruction or exhortation or warning]. But test all things carefully [so you can recognize what is good]. Hold firmly to that which is good."

Whole books have been written on the subject, but I will end with what Paul wrote in 1 Corinthians 14:1 (NKJV): "Pursue love, and desire spiritual gifts, but especially that you may prophesy."

Go ahead and PROPHESY…

Pioneers and Settlers

You have to admit that walking with the Lord is a journey, and there's so much to learn. For example, I can remember in the 1980s beginning to realize that not everyone thought like me.

I was and still am pursuing God even while in reality He has always pursued me. Back then and still now there is a fire, a very deep desire, to see the Kingdom of God not only on the earth but in people's lives. Yet I honestly couldn't understand for years why I felt the way I did.

One day Pastor Tony Saraiva of Christian Life Fellow in Rehoboth, Massachusetts was preaching- perhaps at an elder's meeting- and he made this statement. "You build with some and you build for some." Wow, how true is that.

Then some time shortly after, I heard someone else say that the church is made up of "pioneers and settlers" with the vast majority being settlers. That statement brought such freedom to me and allowed me to see people differently. I had been placing expectations on people that even God didn't put on them, which was very unfair. After this I was able to come to a deeper place of seeing people for who they were and not for who they weren't, or who I even wished them to be.

Pioneers are those who are always exploring the things of God. They are like Lewis & Clark and David Livingstone. David Livingstone once said, "I am prepared to go anywhere, provided it be forward." Perhaps the opening line of the 1966 Star Trek series says it best, "Space: The final frontier These are the voyages of the Starship Enterprise. Its five-year mission, to explore strange new worlds, to seek out new life and new civilizations, to boldly go where no man has gone before."

Pioneering: that inner desire to see God move on the earth and to discover how and when He wants to reveal Himself.

Listen, both pioneers and settlers are important. Pioneers start things. Settlers develop and stabilize them. Just be who you are…

The Natural Mind

We have two minds: a natural mind and a spiritual one. Our challenge is to always make sure we're living in our spiritual mind, or as Paul writes in Philippians 2:5 (NKJV): "Let this mind be in you which was also in Christ Jesus."

What Paul is saying here is that we have a choice to be naturally-minded or spiritually-minded. People often give themselves permission to be carnally-minded because they prefer to live in their flesh, having their own attitudes and doing their own things.

How about us?

The problem with having two minds is that it causes us to be double-minded, and James 1:8 (NKJV) warns us about the fruit/result of that. He writes that a double-minded man is "unstable in all his ways."

Honestly, we have to get sick and tired of being sick and tired.

Not only does it cause us to be unstable in every area of our lives but also prohibits us from receiving the things of the Spirit. Very often we're frustrated because we can't hear or discern what the Holy Spirit is saying. Let's see what Paul says to us about being naturally-minded.

1 Corinthians 2:14 (NKJV): "But the natural man does not receive the things of the Spirit of God, for they are foolishness to him; nor can he know them, because they are spiritually discerned."

Romans 8:5-7 (NKJV): "For those who live according to the flesh set their minds on the things of the flesh, but those who live according to the Spirit, the things of the Spirit. For to be carnally minded is death, but to be spiritually minded is life and peace. Because the carnal mind is enmity against God; for it is not subject to the law of God, nor indeed can be."

When we give ourselves permission to be naturally/carnally minded we are actually at war with God. So the question is why we allow ourselves to live in our natural mind…

When Your Tragedies Become Your Treasures

How many times in your life have you felt like "Humpty Dumpty," that character in the old 1700s nursery rhyme? The depiction is one of a shattered life.

"Humpty Dumpty had a great fall.

All the king's horses and all the king's men

Couldn't put Humpty together again."

I recall feeling this way on more than one occasion. During these times even taking a breath was painful, and I wasn't sure I could face another day. I won't go into details, but here are a few: the day and days following my brother Craig's death at the hands of a drunk driver, watching Donna miscarry two of our children who are now in heaven, my living on a hardwood floor for 3.5 years after 2000 pounds had fallen on my back.

I had no idea how I would make it through those particular days, never mind the days after that. Yet I can tell you I learned so much during those times of great pain and darkness, among other things that as Peter says, I am "kept by the power of God." (1 Peter 1:5, NKJV)

Indeed my tragedies have become my treasures.

And what I learned can never be stolen from me. These events have shaped my life and God has revealed Himself to me in so many intimate and personal ways that like Job I can say, "For I know that my Redeemer lives." (Job 19:25, NKJV)

One of the biggest treasures I have been given is to really know the dwelling place of God. For many years I was satisfied with visitations of

God but knew there was more. I hungered for it and then discovered Isaiah 57:15 (NKJV): "For thus says the High and Lofty One Who inhabits eternity, whose name is Holy: 'I dwell in the high and holy place, with him who has a contrite and humble spirit, To revive the spirit of the humble, And to revive the heart of the contrite ones.' " The Hebrew word for broken and contrite is "shabar," which means to be shattered into little pieces.

For all of you who have known and will experience tragedies, the greatest treasure you will find is knowing and experiencing the dwelling place of God.

Where's Tinker Bell?

I am showing my age. Tinker Bell is a fairy made famous by Walt Disney in movies and cartoons. Tinker Bell sprinkles pixie dust to create magical moments.

But why the question "Where is she? Where's Tinker Bell?"

First let me say that I love all the gifts of the Holy Spirt and the atmosphere that is created by the presence of God. I love when God shows up and manifests His love and power. I love when the prophetic anointing is present and when within seconds prophetic words literally change lives.

I am fully persuaded that God is always present. The challenge becomes discerning His presence and discovering what He wants to do in our lives, especially in a corporate meeting of believers.

That being said I have seen the danger of people being so hungry to see God move that they lose sight of the character and holiness of God and therefore reduce the Holy Spirit to Tinker Bell. They are looking for "hocus pocus/abracadabra" - some sort of magical words that will create a kind of supernatural moment.

As a prophetic person I cannot begin to count the times I'm approached by people looking for a prophetic word. People are often subtle, but nevertheless they want a word from God. Sometimes I feel like "Aladdin's Lamp," where my forehead is rubbed to see what comes out. This can also happen at church services where because of the strong desire for God to move, the service gets turned into a bizarre event.

We have to be careful we don't create a strange fire, or as Leviticus 10:1 says, a "Profane Fire."

Let's not reduce the Holy Spirit to Tinker Bell!

The School of Sovereignty

In Psalm 46:4 (NKJV) it says, "There is a river whose streams shall make glad the city of God." Picture with me a river, and like with most rivers, it's created by the coming together of several streams of varying sizes.

There are several expressions or movements in the church today. Each movement I call a stream, and each of these vary in size. There is the evangelical stream, as well as the pentecostal and charismatic streams. There are Faith Churches, conservative churches, liberal churches, Black, Hispanic, Latino, and Haitian churches or streams. And remember that all of these merge into one river, and that river makes God happy.

While I've mentioned several streams (and there are thousands more), I have neglected to mention the particular stream I am from. While I am part of a charismatic/pentecostal church, the steam I most identify with is the stream called Sovereignty.

"The sovereignty of God means that He has total control of all things past, present, and future. Nothing happens that is out of His knowledge and control. All things are either caused by Him or allowed by Him for His own purposes and through His perfect will and timing." (www.GotQuestions.org)

Easton's Bible Dictionary defines God's Sovereignty as His "absolute right to do all things according to his own good pleasure."

My definition: God is ultimately in control of everything. Nothing happens that He is not aware of and has not allowed. Though I don't understand and at times don't like it, I fully accept that God is perfect. In Psalm 18:30 and 2 Samuel 22:31(NKJV) it says, "As for God, His way is perfect."

While there are many streams (denominations), and there have been many moves of God's Spirit in different locations around the world, I am looking most especially for the river mentioned in Revelation 22: 1-2 (NKJV).

"And he showed me a pure river of water of life, clear as crystal, proceeding from the throne of God and of the Lamb. In the middle of its street, and on either side of the river, was the tree of life, which bore twelve fruits, each tree yielding its fruit every month. The leaves of the tree were for the healing of the nations."

No matter the river, my true origin is the School of Sovereignty...

Learning to Be Wise

You can ask my wife about when I first became a believer and even for many years after, I would talk and talk and talk but rarely listen to people. Over time I discovered that I used to offend people when I talked on and on. I am still realizing that when people talk and talk and don't really listen, it's a reflection of not assigning value to the other person or to their message.

We can say to someone that we love them, but the question becomes, "Am I demonstrating it?"

Here are a few verses that have helped transform my life:

James 1:19 (AMP) "Understand this, my beloved brothers and sisters. Let everyone be quick to hear [be a careful, thoughtful listener], slow to speak [a speaker of carefully chosen words and], slow to anger [patient, reflective, forgiving]."

It says be quick to hear, be a careful, thoughtful listener, and choose your words carefully. These are such critical things for all of our relationships.

Add to that:

Proverbs 10:19 (NKJV): "In the multitude of words sin is not lacking, But he who restrains his lips is wise." and then from (ERV): "A person who talks too much gets into trouble. A wise person learns to be quiet."

Proverbs 17:28 (NKJV): "Even a fool is counted wise when he holds his peace; When he shuts his lips, he is considered perceptive."

I've just given away my secret. Everyone thinks (well, perhaps not everyone) that I am so wise, but I have people fooled; I've just learned to keep my mouth shut.

The other thing I've learned - how precious people are.

The Promise of Exodus 33

When you come across a promise from God you must seize it and never let it be stolen. The following two promises will change your life forever.

Picture for a moment God speaking to Moses and telling him that when he came into the promised land that He'd send His angel to drive out the enemies living there. Verse 2 of Exodus 33, "And I will send My Angel before you, and I will drive out the Canaanite and the Amorite and the Hittite and the Perizzite and the Hivite and the Jebusite…" He goes on to say, "Go up to a land flowing with milk and honey; for I will not go up in your midst."

Remember what God says here. He says He won't go with them.

It has to be during Moses' time with God in the Tabernacle of Meeting when the conversation about the promised land continues. We find Moses asking God a question. Verse 12: "Then Moses said to the Lord, 'See, You say to me, "Bring up this people." But You have not let me know whom You will send with me.' "

Remember that God had already told him he wasn't going, so what was left to know was who He was sending with him.

God responds to Moses, "My Presence will go with you, and I will give you rest." I love Moses' response. "Then he (Moses) said to Him, 'If Your Presence does not go with us, do not bring us up from here.' " (Exodus 33:14)

Wow… He says in effect, "If you don't go; I am not going." God's response? "My Presence will go with you, and I will give you rest." (verse 15)

Wait. Did you see that? The promise is that God's presence will be with us, and get ready for this, that God will give us rest. Wait. He WILL GIVE US REST?

It reminds me of Hebrews four where God says that the children of Israel failed to enter the rest because they didn't mix faith with what they heard. Let's not make the same mistake.

As I pondered the promise of rest, God spoke to me and said, "Man was created for rest." He reminded me that man was created on the sixth day, and his first day on the earth was the seventh day, or the day of rest.

One final thing you need to know is that when man was created, he was created to walk with God in the Garden of Eden. The Hebrew meaning of Eden is "presence." We were created to live in His presence and to have rest.

So today and tomorrow and the day after you have this eternal promise - God will go with you and you can have rest...

Will we really seize what we were promised and created for?

The First Question in the Bible

Genesis 3:9: "Then the Lord God called to Adam and said to him, 'Where are you?' "

I think we can all admit that we get that question fairly often. We might not get it in our ears, but for sure we've heard it in our Spirit. I can see us calling to our children - honey, where are you? And we're on the cell phone asking the same question. It seems simple enough.

The timing of the question biblically is directly after Adam and Eve go into hiding because of their sin. That seems to be our normal response to sin – rather than running TO God, we hide or run away.

Adam's response to the question is in verse 10: "I heard Your voice in the garden, and I was afraid because I was naked; and I hid myself."

He's still hearing God even though he has sinned. God is still pursuing us in spite of our wrongdoing. He simply wants us to be accountable rather than hiding and giving excuses, which often amount to blaming other people.

Adam's response leads to God's next two questions. Verse 11: "Who told you that you were naked? Have you eaten from the tree of which I commanded you that you should not eat?"

Adam responds by saying, verse 12: "The woman whom You gave to be with me, she gave me of the tree, and I ate." God's response: "And the Lord God said to the woman, 'What is this you have done?' The woman said, 'The serpent deceived me, and I ate.'"

The result of their sin and failure to take responsibility was that they were removed from the garden. I have often wondered what God's response would've been if they'd taken full responsibility for their actions.

I'm not sure what the consequence would have been (if any), but I know they would have found immediate forgiveness. 1 John 1:9 (NKJV): "If we confess our sins, He is faithful and just to forgive us our sins and to cleanse us from all unrighteousness."

What if Adam and Eve had confessed their sin? Would they have been as we are, recipients of grace? "For as the heavens are high above the earth, So great is His mercy toward those who fear Him." (Psalm 103:11, NKJV)

If you hear, "Where are you?" don't hide or run from your Father. Instead run TO Him. Psalm 130:4 (NKJV): "But there is forgiveness with You, That You may be feared."

Where are YOU?

The Genesis Principle

The Genesis principle is that we can't hold people accountable if they don't know what they're accountable for.

We say to our teenager "Don't be late" as we hand them the keys to the car. They say "Okay" and skip out the door. At 11:10PM we find ourselves furiously staring at our watches because our child is not home yet. At 11:55PM our child comes bouncing into the house with a big smile on their face. The first words out of our mouths are, "You're late and you're grounded."

We have just held someone accountable who didn't clearly know what we expected from them. I used to make this mistake all the time. But how could someone know my expectations if I hadn't made it clear?

One day the Holy Spirit asked me what He'd done in Genesis with Adam and Eve. I went back and read the account of their sin in the garden. There in Genesis 3:11 when God was confronting them over their sin, He asked them, "Have you eaten from the tree of which I commanded you that you should not eat?"

There it is: Adam and Eve knew what they were unaccountable for. As I mused with the Lord over this He told me that it was one of the primary principles that He established from the beginning. As I continued to spend time on it I felt led to call this "The Genesis Principle." This means we can't hold people accountable based on an assumption of what we think they know or should know...

As part of the Genesis Principle I saw the need to teach and train people before I held them accountable. Isn't that what God did?

(As a not-so-small aside, on different occasions in the past I've approached people to ask their forgiveness for my violating this principle.)

Hearing God

So much has been written about how to hear God it would take several books just to begin to touch the surface of this topic. A number of years ago I was invited to attend a Power and Love conference in Pennsylvania. During one of the meetings I heard this awesome nugget.

The speaker turned to Isaiah 21:3 and noted how Isaiah heard the Lord speak to him in three distinct ways. Isaiah felt it, he heard it, and he saw it. What a great revelation that is - so true.

To be honest though I'm not fond of the "feeling" thing. This can come when there's a need for healing in a particular part of the body and that part of the body will then feel something. This is akin to a pain in the heart signifying that the person has either a physical problem or something else where pain is manifest.

Here is Isaiah 21:3 (NKJV): "Therefore my loins are filled with pain; Pangs have taken hold of me, like the pangs of a woman in labor. I was distressed when I heard it; I was dismayed when I saw it."

Lessons from Extraordinary People in Transition

It was perhaps six years ago when our church (Solomon's Porch) was asked to participate in helping run the overflow overnight homeless shelter in the city of Fall River, Massachusetts. The City had its normal, everyday shelter, but in the winter the number of people who needed nightly shelter more than doubled. What started as our volunteering as a church group eventually turned into our directing the whole winter program.

I can remember my attitude when we first committed to helping the homeless. My thought was that WE were going to help/minister to them. It was probably during the first week however, when I realized that the opposite was true: that these wonderful people were actually ministering to us.

The Lord used these PEOPLE, (the idea of calling them "homeless" devalues who they are) to minister to and change me. First and foremost, these are people. I hadn't seen them as people. The circumstances leading to their homelessness are often unfair, and if not for the grace of God I could easily see myself in their situation. For example, I remember being out of work for three and half years after suffering a back injury and at one point being eight months behind in my mortgage. Had God not intervened I would have been in their same position.

Like me, some of them had been injured, and because they couldn't work had eventually lost their home or apartment. Others had gone through a family crisis and had had a breakdown. Others were betrayed by their husband or their wife. And yes, there were drug and alcohol problems. The list goes on, but the point is...THEY ARE PEOPLE...

From that point forward, I just hated calling them or hearing them referred to as homeless people. The Lord showed me one day that in reality, they are "extraordinary people in transition."

That's who they are: EXTRAORDINARY PEOPLE IN TRANSITION.

For the six years we worked with them the Lord taught me many lessons. I have indeed been changed by these extraordinary people.

Grasshopper Mentality

When the spies returned from scoping out the promised land, they were jubilant about the land itself and also about the fruits and vegetables. The grapes alone took two men to carry. Numbers 33:21 (NKJV): "Then they came to the Valley of Eshcol, and there cut down a branch with one cluster of grapes; they carried it between two of them on a pole."

"But" - the famous "BUT" that confronts us all - verse 31 says, "But the men who had gone up with him said, 'We are not able to go up against the people, for they are stronger than we.' " They continued to say, verses 32-33: "And they gave the children of Israel a bad report of the land which they had spied out, saying, 'The land through which we have gone as spies is a land that devours its inhabitants, and all the people whom we saw in it are men of great stature. There we saw the giants (the descendants of Anak came from the giants); and we were like grasshoppers in our own sight, and so we were in their sight.' "

Think for a moment about all the miraculous things they had already seen - the plagues in Egypt, the Red Sea being opened, and Pharaoh's army being destroyed, to name but a few. Over and over God did miracle after miracle, yet when it came time to seize the promises that God had for them, what do they do? They see the giants and immediately forget everything God had done for them. They see themselves as small, inferior, and insignificant. They had "grasshopper mentality." Do we do the same thing? Do we focus on our "giants" and not on our "God?"

In verse 30 Caleb is pleading with them, saying in essence, "We can do this thing." "Let us go up at once and take possession, for we are well able to overcome it." Sadly, the voice of ten men caused all of the Israelites to wander for 40 years. They saw the giants as bigger and stronger than God.

This GRASSHOPPER MENTALITY caused them to miss what God had promised and planned for them.

Do we have GRASSHOPPER MENTALITY?

Help is on the Way

In Daniel chapter ten we find that Daniel has been fasting for three weeks to seek understanding of a vision God had given him. The angel Gabriel was trying to help Daniel, but verse 13 says there was opposition: "But the prince of the kingdom of Persia withstood me twenty-one days." The demonic hindrance didn't allow Daniel to understand, even with the help of Gabriel.

All this to say that we shouldn't think it strange if Satan tries to hinder us. First Peter 4:12 (NKJV): "Beloved, do not think it strange concerning the fiery trial which is to try you, as though some strange thing happened to you."

When Gabriel isn't successful fighting the Prince of Persia, God sends Michael to assist him. Now the rest of verse 13: "...and behold, Michael, one of the chief princes, came to help me, for I had been left alone there with the kings of Persia."

There have been numerous times in my life when I have heard God say to me, "Help is on the way."

Whatever you're facing or going to face, God will do whatever it takes to battle on your behalf. Psalm 57:3 (NKJV): "He shall send from heaven and save me."

Hear me and remember - HELP IS ON THE WAY...

You Were Born for Greatness

Dear Jesus, please help us understand who we are and help us to stop focusing on who we are not. We have been beguiled, tricked, deceived, hoodwinked, blinded, and lied to.

Yet the reality is... each one of us is so amazing. We've somehow settled for ordinary lives when all along the plan for us has been extraordinary. We're stuck in our "ruts and routines." Why is this?

Here is what God spoke to Daniel, "The people who know their God shall be strong, and carry out great exploits." (Daniel 11:32, NKJV) The message is not just to Daniel but is spoken to everyone who knows God. It says YOU WILL BE STRONG AND CARRY OUT GREAT, GREAT EXPLOITS.

Deuteronomy 28:13 (NCV) says, "The Lord will make you like the head and not like the tail; you will be on top and not on bottom."

Yes, you were born for greatness, Jeremiah 1:5 (MSG): "Before I shaped you in the womb, I knew all about you. Before you saw the light of day, I had holy plans for you." Not just ordinary plans but holy plans. Notice its plural.

I enjoy watching the various talent shows from all over the world, because we because we get to see ordinary people display extraordinary gifts. Kathleen Jenkins is a case in point. Kathleen is a 25 year-old British woman who cleaned toilets for a living until one day she mustered the courage to audition for "Britain's Got Talent." She wowed the judges but continued to clean toilets until she finished as runner up and was able to sign a singing contract. Kathleen is a snapshot of your potential.

Can you hear what Jesus said to the man in the temple who had a withered hand? What was the answer for the infirmity? Mark 3:3 (NKJV): "And He said to the man who had the withered hand, ' Step forward.' "

Go ahead; step forward....

Intimidation

How many times in all of our lives have we been intimidated and kept prisoner from being all that God has ordained us to be?

In Jeremiah chapter one we see the word of the Lord going to Jeremiah telling him that he was called and set apart before he was born. It's easy to see that for Jeremiah, easy to see that for other people, but can you believe that about yourself? Though the words were spoken to Jeremiah, God is speaking them to all of you too. From the Message

Bible, "Before I shaped you in the womb, I knew all about you. Before you saw the light of day, I had holy plans for you." (Jeremiah 1:5)

But then as with Jeremiah, the excuses begin, verse six: "Then said I: 'Ah, Lord God! Behold, I cannot speak, for I am a youth.' " God's response is in verses 7-8 (NKJV), "But the Lord said to me: 'Do not say, "I am a youth," For you shall go to all to whom I send you, And whatever I command you, you shall speak. Do not be afraid of their faces, For I am with you to deliver you,' says the Lord."

One of the excuses I hear all the time is "I'm not anointed." Well, 1 John 2:20 (NKJV) clearly says that you already have an anointing: "But you have an anointing from the Holy One."

STOP WITH THE EXCUSES... Stop looking at who you're not and start looking at who you are. Stop with the negative self-talk, and realize you were born to be God's son or daughter and His servant. Listen, God says, I AM WITH YOU.

The days of your intimidation are over...

Goliath Had A Brother

All of us have had Goliaths in our lives.

Goliaths represent giant obstacles, sins, or weaknesses which perpetually harass and threaten us.

In 1 Samuel 17, day after day Goliath would threaten, harass, and challenge the men in the army of Israel until one day David finally kills him.

Isn't it true that day after day we too are being harassed and challenged by our personal Goliaths? What a great day it is when the giant we've been battling is finally dealt with.

We're happy until... the one day that the giant we thought we'd defeated reappears. "What's this?" we ask. "I defeated my Goliath, yet here he is again." We become discouraged thinking that we'll never be free. We may even think that we never defeated him in the first place. The situation can become so overwhelming that it undermines our faith and especially the power that is in Christ.

I can recall one day when the Goliath that I thought I had killed reappeared alive and well. I began to ask God all the questions. Why, how come, what didn't I do, what do I need to do, etcetera.

In the meantime, while I was working this out with the Lord, I went through a period of time when I was getting hammered on a regular basis. One day I heard the voice of God say, "Goliath had a brother." (2 Samuel 21:19) I was reassured that I had killed my giant but knew then that he had a relative.

Not knowing where in the Bible it spoke of Goliath's brother, I googled it and found 1 Chronicles 20:5 (NKJV): "Again there was war with the Philistines, and Elhanan the son of Jair killed Lahmi the brother of Goliath the Gittite, the shaft of whose spear was like a weaver's beam."

What a great day that was, because it assured me that I had eliminated my giant and that I would likewise eliminate any brother, cousin, nephew, step brother, or any other giant that would come into my life.

Goliath had a brother and he's dead too…

I'm Not Coming Off the Wall

We find Nehemiah busy rebuilding the wall surrounding Jerusalem. And in the midst of it, using various methods, others are trying to stop him.

This isn't surprising in Nehemiah's story nor should it be surprising for us. When we are trying to serve the Lord and accomplish things for the Kingdom of God, our enemy will use whatever is at his disposal to discourage and stop us.

Such is the case with Nehemiah 6:1-2 (NKJV): "Now it happened when Sanballat, Tobiah, Geshem the Arab, and the rest of our enemies heard that I had rebuilt the wall, and that there were no breaks left in it (though at that time I had not hung the doors in the gates), that Sanballat and Geshem sent to me, saying, 'Come, let us meet together among the villages in the plain of Ono.' But they thought to do me harm."

What a great picture of one of our enemy's devices. He wants us to engage in conversations that have no purpose except to hurt us. Did you notice the name of the plain they wanted to meet in? It's the plain of "ONO" as in "Oh no, I am not going to talk with you!"

We need to adopt and embrace the attitude of Nehemiah as he responds in

Nehemiah 6:3 (NKJV): "So I sent messengers to them, saying, 'I am doing a great work, so that I cannot come down. Why should the work cease while I leave it and go down to you?' "

It would be wonderful if it was necessary to say no only once, but suffice to say again that our enemy is relentless; he tries us and wears us down. Verse four says, "But they sent me this message four times, and I answered them in the same manner."

Stay consistent; don't reason or waver.

YOU'RE DOING A GREAT WORK FOR THE LORD… It's vital that you assign Holy Ghost VALUE to what God has called you to do… You're building an everlasting Kingdom…

Beyond Evangelism

I have a confession to make.

For as long as I can remember I have disliked the term evangelism. It's always sounded mechanical to me rather than resembling something that originates from the heart. In fact, the whole idea of "winning" souls sounds like a competition. In the 70s and 80s people would stand on street corners and hand out "chic" tracs, most of which seemed designed to send people to hell if they didn't repeat a prayer of salvation.

People by the thousands would pray a prayer accepting Christ because doing so would prevent them from going to hell. They would pray a prayer of repentance, but too often it was only words. After they prayed it they were told, "You now are saved." There was no talk of continuing to walk in a way that was pleasing to the Lord. It was "Pray this and now you're saved." I can remember people evangelizing on weekends, and at weekend's end they would compare how many people they got to pray.

Forgive me, but it felt like collecting "scalps."

Thankfully something happened in the Spirit. God began showing us the depth of Luke 14:22-24. The Amplified Bible says, "And the servant [after returning] said, 'Sir, what you commanded has been done, and still there is room.' Then the master told the servant, 'Go out into the highways and along the hedges, and compel them to come in, so that my house may be filled [with guests].' " In one translation it says, "Compel the guests of honor to come."

I just love the heart behind this translation. As we look into the highways and by-ways there are precious people who the Spirit calls "guests of honor." We are to pour our hearts into these people so they'll feel loved and honored and will come running to the marriage feast. Can you hear the heart of the Father? I want my house to be filled...

Have you heard the cry? Listen, you are needed!

Where Are You, God?

Have you ever felt like God was listening to everyone but you? Answering everyone else's prayer but not yours? There've been a few times when I've believed that the Lord was on vacation in Bermuda.

A number of Psalms express the despair we may feel in those moments. David expresses his by asking, "How long will you hide your face from me?" In fact, four times in this psalm David asks, "How long?" Verse one says, "How long, O Lord? Will You forget me forever? How long will You hide Your face from me?" (Psalm 13:1, NKJV)

When you research this Psalm there is no background as to why it was written. Yet as we look at David's life we know that he often found himself struggling with his relationship with God. Can you relate?

Then there is Psalm 22:1 (NKJV): "My God, My God, why have You forsaken Me? Why are You so far from helping Me, And from the words of My groaning?" Yes, there are times that we feel that God has abandoned us, or at best, is disinterested. Thankfully, this is only a feeling and not a reality.

In these times of despair and depression the enemy of our soul is lurking. It is during these times that you and I can cling to 1 Samuel 12:22 (NKJV): "For the Lord will not forsake His people, for His great name's sake, because it has pleased the Lord to make you His people."

We are HIS PEOPLE... We are his "kids." This is lovingly stated to Isaiah. Isaiah 49:15 (CEV): "The Lord answered, 'Could a mother forget a child who nurses at her breast? Could she fail to love an infant who came from her own body? Even if a mother could forget, I will never forget you.' "

Where are you God? I am right here.

Lessons from the Four Lepers

In 1 Kings 7 we find that Israel is at war with Syria, and in the process they erect a blockade which causes a severe famine in Samaria. We find four lepers who are at the entrance of the gate of the city (verse 3): "...and they said to one another, 'Why are we sitting here until we die?' " Verse 4: "If we say, 'We will enter the city,' the famine is in the city, and we shall die there. And if we sit here, we die also.' "

It seems like the four have no good options, which seems true for us sometimes. If we do nothing we'll die (in a manner of speaking), yet if we return to our old familiar ways, we'll also perish.

In their case they realized something had to be done. They could neither sit and do nothing, nor could they go back; they had to take a risk and see what God might do. In this case they decide to surrender to the Syrian army. The worst thing that could have happened is that they'd be killed. So the lepers approach the enemy camp only to find it has been abandoned with everything left behind - food, water, clothing, silver and gold. The lepers start hoarding everything and then realize they can share the provision that the enemy's abandoned.

There are times we just don't know what to do, and all we can hope for is mercy and a miracle. In this case God's provision was in the enemy's camp. I am convinced that, like in Ezra six when King Darius writes a decree that what Nebuchadnezzar had stolen from the Temple had to be given back, this is true for us too. I believe that a decree has been written in heaven, and whatever the enemy has stolen from the church (you), he has to give back.

The lepers discovered that God's provision wasn't in doing nothing or returning to the familiar, but right in the enemy's camp.

You might want to pose the same question the four lepers did and then take a risk and trust God. Why? Because there is no life in doing nothing and no life in returning to the past.

Maybe We Need A Good "Dope" Slap

We know that a "dope" slap is normally an affectionate, gentle slap across a person's head which in effect says, "Wake up!"

In Acts 12 we find this very situation. Peter has been arrested and put into prison, and on one particular night he's sleeping in chains between two guards. Two other guards watch his prison door. And in verse five it says constant prayer is offered to God for him. Verse 7 (NKJV) says, "Now behold, an angel of the Lord stood by him, and a light shone in the prison; and he struck Peter on the side and raised him up, saying, 'Arise quickly!' And his chains fell off his hands."

Did you picture that in your mind? Peter is in prison; sleeping in chains between two guards. An angel shows up and Peter continues to sleep. The angel has to give him a slap on the side of his head in order to get his attention, in essence saying, "Come on, Peter! You have to wake up so you can get out of here."

Perhaps Peter had grown comfortable in prison and in his chains.

We have to be careful that we don't do the same. It is much like many wonderful people in Romania. They were under a communist regime for 25 years and the day came when the government was overthrown. Though Romanians are free, many of them are still imprisoned in the way they think. Many of them are just stuck and could really use an angelic slap.

If you notice, as soon as the angel slaps Peter, all his chains fall off and he walks out of prison past the guards. Verse eight says, "Arise quickly!' And his chains fell off his hands." Did you see the admonition to "arise quickly?" When the Holy Spirit brings freedom, you don't want to hang around where you have been, but move out quickly.

I can hear the voice of the Holy Spirit quote Joel 3:9 (NKJV): "Wake up the mighty men." Yes, it's time we wake out of slumber. Proverbs 6:9 (NKJV): "How long will you slumber, O sluggard? When will you rise from your sleep?"

There is a great work to be done, and the church has to wake up…

I Don't Need Your Help

Gideon was told to drive the Midianites out of Israel. The Midianite army consisted of 135,00 troops, while Gideon's army consisted of 32,000 men. How do you like those odds? Gideon had to be thinking that the whole thing was nuts.

God has a word for him, though. "And the Lord said to Gideon, 'The people who are with you are too many for Me to give the Midianites into their hands, lest Israel claim glory for itself against Me, saying, 'My own hand has saved me.' " (Judges 7:2, NKJV)

God tells him that He doesn't need his help defeating the Midianites and furthermore doesn't want him taking the credit after they win. This could be our situation. If we're honest, there have been occasions when we've been tempted in the same way to take credit for something miraculous in our life. In reality, though, even the anointing we have is not our own, but His.

Gideon gathers his army and tells those who are afraid to "go home." Twenty-two thousand go home, leaving 10,000 men. What do you suppose was going through Gideon's mind? He had to have been thinking that the whole thing was crazy.

Then God comes again with another word. Verse four: "But the Lord said to Gideon, 'The people are still too many.' " His army is then reduced to 300 men, and God finally tells him that he is ready!

The message is clear: "I don't need your help." We see this said in another way in Zachariah 4:6 (NKJV): "This is the word of the Lord to Zerubbabel: 'Not by might nor by power, but by My Spirit.' "

Whatever you're facing in your life right now I bet you're examining and wondering what you can do. Perhaps you can do this or perhaps that. What if we the church really live our lives fully dependent on what God alone can do? In Jeremiah 17:5 (NKJV) we read, "Thus says the Lord: 'Cursed is the man who trusts in man And makes flesh his strength.' "

I can hear God say to all of us - I DON'T NEED YOUR HELP...

Tell Peter

It's early in the morning; Jesus is dead and has been placed in the tomb. The women go to the tomb in hopes of anointing his body. Back in the upper room Peter has to be grieving with guilt. I can't imagine the pain he's in.

When they get to the tomb we read Mark 16: 5-7 (NKJV): "And entering the tomb, they saw a young man clothed in a long white robe sitting on the right side; and they were alarmed. But he said to them, 'Do not be alarmed. You seek Jesus of Nazareth, who was crucified. He is risen! He is not here. See the place where they laid Him. But go, tell His disciples—AND PETER—that He is going before you into Galilee; there you will see Him, as He said to you.' "

Can we comprehend the love and affection that the Lord had for Peter in that particular moment? Essentially God was saying to Peter, "Hey Peter, I love you and I know the pain you are in. I will see you shortly in Galilee." There was no condemnation, no statement saying "You failed me." Just a simple phrase saying "Tell Peter I was asking for him."

Verse eight tells us that the women left the tomb, "So they went out quickly and fled from the tomb, for they trembled and were amazed." When they tell Peter his response was that of John - HE RAN TO THE TOMB...

My heart is joy-filled to know that the Lord had the angel say, "Tell Peter I said hello." My heart bursts with joy knowing that at the times I fail, Jesus still wants a relationship with me. His love for me and you DOES NOT CHANGE... In fact, Jesus addresses Peter's failure in Luke 22:32 (ESV): "but I have prayed for you that your faith may not fail. And when you have turned again, strengthen your brothers."

Take your failures and use them to strengthen others in their walk...Tell Peter I'm asking for him/you...

Compelled

Compelled means feeling forced or obligated to do something. Being compelled by the Holy Spirit is a powerful incentive that facilitates the purposes of God. Being compelled by our flesh/emotions, on the other hand, is often a disaster.

It's critical that in the days ahead we discern whether we're being compelled by the Holy Spirit or our flesh. We can have the right heart and the right incentive but the absolute wrong timing. The story of Abraham and Sarah comes to mind. When they're unable to have a child, they feel compelled to fulfill their destiny and prophetic word another way. The result was Ishmael's birth. Even to this day the consequences of their action are still felt.

There is also the time when Saul wants to engage the Philistines in warfare but has to wait for Samuel to present an offering to the Lord. It's agreed that Samuel will come back in seven days, but when he doesn't, Saul takes it upon himself to bring forth the burnt offering. Listen to Saul's logic as Samuel asks him why he didn't wait, and you'll see the consequences of "feeling compelled." Being compelled must be aligned with biblical order and right timing, or consequences ensue.

Here's the account given in 1 Samuel 13:11-13 (NKJV): "And Samuel said, 'What have you done?' " Can we hear that? "Saul said, 'When I saw (he saw with his natural eyes) that the people were scattered from me (trusting in his army rather than trusting in God), and that you did not come within the days appointed, and that the Philistines gathered together at Michmash, then I said, "The Philistines will now come down on me at Gilgal, and I have not made supplication to the Lord." Therefore I felt compelled, and offered a burnt offering.' " "And Samuel said to Saul, 'You have done foolishly. You have not kept the commandment of the Lord your God, which He commanded you. For now the Lord would have established your kingdom over Israel forever. But now your kingdom shall not continue.' "

Then we're given the account in Acts 18 when Paul and Silas have come from Macedonia. It says that Paul is compelled by the Spirit and testifies to the Jews that "Jesus is the Christ."

Though it created quite a stir in the city, Paul and Silas were used powerfully to turn a city upside down for the purposes of God.

We must discern the source of our being compelled. Our future depends on it.

Take Away the Noise of Your Songs

In Amos 5:23 we read, "Take away from Me the noise of your songs, For I will not hear the melody of your stringed instruments."

I love to worship but worship must have intent and purpose. The purpose of worship is that we are bringing to God the only thing that is really ours to bring. Everything belongs to the Lord, everything. All the silver, all the gold. So in actuality the only thing that we can bring to God that is ours, is our worship.

Worship has changed dramatically in the past 30 or so years, becoming far more expressive with the introduction of multiple instruments. The word worship is

From Strong's Concordance G4352 (meaning to kiss, like a dog licking his master's hand); to fawn or crouch to, that is, (literally or figuratively) prostrate oneself in homage (do reverence to, adore): - worship.

Worship in the New Testament is mentioned 59 times, and in the book of Revelation we find the word "proskuneo" mentioned 21 times. It's amazing the imagery the scriptures convey about it.

Worship is about Him and not about us… With that being said I believe at times that we fall into the trap of worshipping worship. It's during worship that we're often overwhelmed with peace, joy, and contentment. So just because we're overwhelmed with these emotions at times doesn't mean we're worshipping God, but worshipping so we can feel good.

Another danger I see with the introduction of multiple instruments is a seeming competition between musicians. I've seen worship where it's no longer about worshipping God; it's about whose songs sound better.

I've also been in worship services where the music is so loud that "your ears bleed." (Thankfully this is just an expression, not a reality.) Everyone is having a good time, but you're no longer worshipping; you're at a kind of concert..

Instead of these, worship expressed rightly is meant to honor with extravagant love and extreme submission (Webster's Dictionary, 1828). Psalm 95:6 says, "Oh come, let us worship and bow down; let us kneel before the Lord, our Maker!"

A picture of worship that I love and want to be a part of is in Revelation 4:9: "Whenever the living creatures give glory and honor and thanks to Him who sits on the throne, who lives forever and ever, the twenty-four elders fall down before Him who sits on the throne and worship Him who lives forever and ever, and cast their crowns before the throne, saying: 'You are worthy, O Lord, To receive glory and honor and power; For You created all things, And by Your will they exist and were created.' "

I want to be found worshipping like the living creatures and the twenty-four elders.

So my heart's cry is, "Take away the noise of your songs…"

Have You Met the Man in the Fire?

You're far from home (Israel) and at best, you're a teenager. You're being pressured to compromise your faith by bowing down to worship the golden image, which you refuse to do.

Would we do this? No one is around to see if we compromise. We're lonely, and compromising would be easier than keeping our integrity.

Yet sometimes integrity is the only thing we have. In Daniel 3:18 (NKJV) they tell Nebuchadnezzar, "Let it be known to you, O king, that we do not serve your gods, nor will we worship the gold image which you have set up." The result of their refusal is that they're thrown into a fiery furnace. And there in the fire Jesus dances with them.

Can we also choose the fiery furnace?

I believe that it was more than simple obedience that allowed these three young men to choose the fiery furnace, and that's what they did; they chose the fire. I believe we spend much of our time avoiding the fire when all along that's where God is. He's in the fire...

Have you met the Man in the fire?

Criticism Killed A Revival

In 1904 a revival broke out in Wales. It started with a young man named Evan Roberts who was 26 when revival came. Thirteen years earlier God spoke to Evan that he would be instrumental in bringing revival there.

The lesson here is to cling to your vision, and water it as you would a seed.

During this revival and in just nine months, over 100,000 people committed their lives to Jesus and hundreds of thousands more over the next few years. Things were going well until Evan Roberts started listening to all the voices of criticism. He began to question whether or not he was hearing God.

This is one of the most effective weapons of Satan - criticism.

One of the other components that can shipwreck a move of God is exhaustion. Roberts' meetings lasted into the early morning hours, sometimes for two weeks at a time. Take exhaustion and criticism, and together they're a recipe for disaster. At the same time these things were taking place, a woman named Jesse Penn-Lewis began interjecting her own theology into Roberts' mind along with her negative ideas. Soon Evan Roberts had a breakdown.

This great move of God ended in 1905.

Evan Roberts lived until he was 72, but he stopped preaching in his late twenties. Some things that I have learned from Evan Roberts:

Hold onto your vision

Water what God has told you

Don't be consumed by the voices of criticism

Don't allow other doctrines to fill your mind

Don't become exhausted - be balanced

Burnt Stones

In the beginning of the Book of Nehemiah, Nehemiah is living in captivity and wants to find out what's happening with the people of Jerusalem. He asks Hanani, who's just come from there. It's important no note Nehemiah's reaction to what he's told.

Nehemiah asks Hanani, one of the people who had come to Babylon from Judah, and Hannai replies: "And they said to me, 'The survivors who are left from the captivity in the province are there in great distress and reproach. The wall of Jerusalem is also broken down, and its gates are burned with fire.' " Nehemiah 1:3 (NKJV)

Nehemiah's response, verse four: "So it was, when I heard these words, that I sat down and wept, and mourned for many days; I was fasting and praying before the God of heaven." Nehemiah's heart was broken, and as we read we continue to see his deep love and concern, not only for the people of Judah but also for Jerusalem.

His burden leads to prayer and fasting, after which he asks the King to let him return to Jerusalem. Nehemiah 2:5: "And I said to the king, 'If it pleases the king, and if your servant has found favor in your sight, I ask that you send me to Judah, to the city of my fathers' tombs, that I may rebuild it.' "

The king lets him return, and after he arrives he goes out to survey firsthand the conditions he's facing. Nehemiah 2:13: "Then I arose in the night, I and a few men with me; I told no one what my God had put in my heart to do at Jerusalem; nor was there any animal with me, except the one on which I rode. And I went out by night."

Did you notice it says, "I told no one what my God had put in my heart?" Very often it's unwise to share your dream or vision because people are happy to tell you why it can't be fulfilled. Sharing with others is often like casting pearls before swine. They'll trample the vision and thereby trample you.

It says that Nehemiah "viewed the walls of Jerusalem which were broken down and its gates which were burned with fire" (2:13) and then speaks to the guys in charge, the priests, nobles, and officials. "And then I said to them, 'You see the distress that we are in, how Jerusalem lies waste, and its gates are burned with fire. Come and let us build the wall of Jerusalem, that we may no longer be a reproach.' And I told them of the hand of my God which had been good upon me, and also of the king's words that he had spoken to me. So they said, 'Let us rise up and build.' Then they set their hands to this good work.' " (Nehemiah 2: 17-18)

Many people see burnt stones and "burnt" people, but Nehemiah saw beyond the reality of the conditions he faced. He saw what God wanted to do and stepped toward the obstacles saying, "God's hand is on me." I can't begin to tell you how many times I've heard pastors talking about the people in their church, seeing only their brokenness and shattered lives and very rarely their potential.

We must see God's ability to take broken and burnt-out people and raise them up to be sons and daughters who become His ambassadors.

We have a choice. We can see burnt stones, or we can see what God wants to do. Which will it be?

I Have Nothing

In 2 Kings 4 we find Elisha talking to the widow of a prophet. The prophet has died leaving his wife and sons in debt and with the potential of going to debtors' prison. 2 Kings 4:1 (NKJV): "A certain woman of the wives of the sons of the prophets cried out to Elisha, saying, 'Your servant my husband is dead, and you know that your servant feared the Lord. And the creditor is coming to take my two sons to be his slaves.' "

So Elisha asks, "What shall I do for you?" Tell me, what do you have in the house?" (verse 2) He wants to know what she has by way of beginning to address her financial issues. The widow's response reflects what is often our attitude, "Your maidservant has nothing in the house but a jar of oil."

There it is: I HAVE NOTHING, yet on second thought... I have a little bit of oil (implying that it's probably not worth mentioning). Elisha instructs her to gather a bunch of jars and tells her that God will fill them all - her seed money for solving their problems: "Go, sell the oil and pay your debt; and you and your sons live on the rest." (verse 7)

One of our propensities is to focus on what we don't have rather than what we do. You see, God can work with what we have. It's like when God tells Moses that he's going to use him to deliver the children of Israel from slavery. Moses objects, never imagining they'll listen to him. Exodus 4:1-2 (NKJV): "Then Moses answered and said, 'But suppose they will not believe me or listen to my voice; suppose they say, "The Lord has not appeared to you." So the Lord said to him, 'What is that in your hand?' He said, 'A rod.' "

What do you have?

We must stop looking at what we don't have and realize that God can work powerfully with what we do have. It's the same principle we see with Gideon when he's called to deliver Israel in Judges 6:14 (NKJV): "Then the Lord turned to him and said, 'Go in this might of yours, and you shall save Israel from the hand of the Midianites. Have I not sent you?' "

Yes, GO IN THIS MIGHT OF YOURS. WHAT'S IN YOUR HAND? WHAT'S IN YOUR HOUSE...

I Missed His Presence

Are you surprised by the number of trials God has allowed you to go through? My personal answer is "Yes," even though I'm very familiar with the message of 1 Peter 4:12 (AMP) which says, "Beloved, do not be surprised at the fiery ordeal which is taking place to test you [that is, to test the quality of your faith], as though something strange or unusual were happening to you."

I have to chuckle because it says, "fiery ordeal," and I think all of us can say that at times that's seemed like an understatement. And as much as it says we shouldn't think it strange or unusual, we do.

In Isaiah 43 the Holy Spirit says, WHEN, not IF, you go through something, I want you to know "I am with you." Furthermore, when you go through something else I'll be sure it won't overtake you, and I'll make a way of escape. Read Isaiah 43:1-3: "I have called you by your name; You are Mine. When you pass through the waters, I will be with you; And through the rivers, they shall not overflow you. When you walk through the fire, you shall not be burned, Nor shall the flame scorch you."

For so many years my focus has been on the trials, and I have missed the love and intimacy of the moment. Peter wrote – "Beloved." Isaiah said, "I CALLED YOU BY NAME, YOU ARE MINE." It is during these trials that our Father has been so close, so near, yet in my focusing on the trials, I have missed His presence.

In all these circumstances I didn't really know that I was being shaped and fashioned into His likeness. Yes, he was fulfilling Philippians 2:13 "for it is God who works in you both to will and to do for His good pleasure." Abba was taking the time to make me look like Him.

Even still, I missed HIM. I missed the opportunity to know Him more intimately, to know His love and affection.

We can focus on the trial or we can focus on Him. The picture I get is of an infant crying, and while the Father is trying everything to comfort the baby, no matter what He tries, nothing helps.

I don't want to miss one more moment of my Father's love and comfort in the midst of the fiery trial.

When You See

Joshua has now taken the place of Moses. The children of Israel are poised to cross the Jordon River. With new leadership often comes a new leadership style, which some people can have a difficult time adapting to.

Here is how Joshua chooses to lead. As Israel is camped on this side of the Jordan, he sends instructions through the camp. Joshua 3:2-3: "So it was, after three days, that the officers went through the camp; and they commanded the people, saying, 'When you see the ark of the covenant of the Lord your God, and the priests, the Levites, bearing it, then you shall set out from your place and go after it.' "

What he says is so subtle but so powerful. It could've been written after the day of Pentecost in Acts chapter two. Joshua says, "WHEN YOU SEE THE ARK OF GOD MOVE, IT'S TIME TO MOVE." Paul wrote something similar to this when he said that those who are led by the Spirit are the sons of God.

I realize that Joshua was speaking about the physical moving of the ark, but we can still take this principle and apply it to our own lives, meaning that when we see God moving or doing something, we need to respond to what He's doing in that moment.

Romans 8:14: "For as many as are led by the Spirit of God, these are sons of God.

I find it interesting that Joshua said when "YOU SEE" the ark of the covenant move, then "YOU MOVE." It's not when someone else sees it, it's when YOU SEE God moving. This is a vital distinction, because too often people do things that others do just for the sake of it. The result leads to following someone else's conviction and not their own. The same is true with following someone else's vision as opposed to what God has shown us personally.

Paul writes in Romans 14, "let every man be fully persuaded in his own mind." Notice it says, "fully" persuaded. God is warning us to not live our lives based on the convictions of others. One day when we stand before God, and He asks us why we did this or that, I don't want to have to respond, "Because I saw so and so do it."

WHEN YOU SEE GOD MOVE - THEN YOU MOVE...

I Have Come to Give You Understanding

This phrase has been taken from Daniel chapter nine. Daniel has had a vision, and for three weeks he's seeking and pursuing God for its meaning. Daniel just doesn't jump to a conclusion; instead, rather than presume or assume, he really seeks the mind of God on the matter.

I know sometimes in a state of anxiousness to know, I've drawn conclusions before their time. It's like being given an unknown thousand-piece puzzle and knowing the outcome before it's a quarter completed. For example, I can look at the body of a massive animal in the puzzle and without seeing the face can conclude that it's a hippopotamus, but in reality, once the rest of the puzzle is put together, I can see that it's actually a rhinoceros.

In Daniel's case, after three weeks the angel of the Lord came to give him understanding. "Yes, while I was speaking in prayer, the man Gabriel, whom I had seen in the vision at the beginning, [a]being caused to fly swiftly, reached me about the time of the evening offering. And he informed me, and talked with me, and said, 'Oh Daniel, I have now come forth to give you skill to understand.'" (Daniel 9:21-22, NKJV)

Do we need understanding? Are we willing to seek after it even if it takes time and we're anxious for an answer?

Why does God want to give us understanding? Two verses tell us. First, Daniel 9:23: "At the beginning of your supplications the command went out, and I have come to tell you, for you are greatly beloved; therefore consider the matter, and understand the vision." We learn that God sends the answer the very first moment Daniel prays because Daniel is "greatly" loved by the Lord. The second verse is Hebrews 11:6 (NKJV): "But without faith it is impossible to please

Him, for he who comes to God must believe that He is, and that He is a rewarder of those who diligently seek Him." God rewards people who are diligent to seek His ways and His heart.

Be confident and know that He has come "to give you understanding."

Are You Hiding?

There are lots of reasons why we hide. Adam and Eve hid from God because they had sinned. Genesis 3:10 (NKJV): "So he said, 'I heard Your voice in the garden, and I was afraid because I was naked; and I hid myself.' " When we sin, our tendency is to hide from God rather than to run to Him.

Another reason we hide from God is seen in the story of Samuel when Samuel comes to Mizpah to anoint Saul as King. They can't find him though, because he's hiding. Samuel 10:22 (NKJV) says of Saul that he is "hidden among the equipment."

Why is Saul hiding? Because earlier when Samuel is speaking with Saul, Samuel is speaking to him with honor and respect. Given Saul's lowly position, he doesn't expect to be treated this way. Daniel 9:21: "And Saul answered and said, 'Am I not a Benjamite, of the smallest of the tribes of Israel, and my family the least of all the families of the tribe of Benjamin? Why then do you speak like this to me?' "

What was Saul's problem? Saul didn't know how to handle respect. He had a poor self-image, an inaccurate perspective of himself. That shouldn't shock anyone because most people are just like Saul, seeing who they're not, instead of who they are.

When we fail to see ourselves as God sees us, we'll hide from the call of God on our lives, or at best, minimize that calling.

Are you hiding?

Consider Your Ways

Twice in chapter one of the book of Haggai we see God speaking to His people. He says to them, "Now therefore, thus says the Lord of hosts: 'Consider your ways!' " He goes on to say, "You have sown much, and bring in little; You eat, but do not have enough; You drink, but you are not filled with drink; You clothe yourselves, but no one is warm; And he who earns wages, Earns wages to put into a bag with holes." (NKJV, verses 5 and 7)

God is asking His children to reflect on their lives and what they're doing. He basically says, look, "Let's be truthful. You're working very hard, but if you're honest with yourselves, you're not getting ahead. Why is that?"

It's really important that we continually take a personal inventory of our lives and as best we can, be brutally honest with ourselves. God asks the question twice in three verses because He wants to get our attention.

Here in the book of Haggai God is asking this question because for sixteen years the people have stopped building the house of God. Why? Because they're thinking something to the effect of, "What I really need to do is take my time and money and take care of my own life."

Perhaps that's something the Holy Spirit is trying to say to some of us. God's saying, take a peek at your life. You're working very hard but it's not getting you ahead. Not at all.

The only way we can change is to recognize there's a need for change. Sometimes we're just stuck doing and doing, but it's all for naught. Is it time for change?

In our personal inventory-taking, we have to be careful we aren't being too hard on ourselves. Some people easily go to, "I'm so displeasing to the Lord. I never do anything right," etcetera. Satan loves to take what God wants us to do in our lives and distort everything and discourage us. If God is asking us to consider our lives, it's possible He's saying, "Listen, you're stuck, and I have so much more for you."

Is this where you are?

In Acts 3:19 it says "Repent (have a change of mind/heart) that times (seasons) of refreshing can come from the presence of God." Could you use a time when God refreshes you?

If God is saying "CONSIDER YOUR WAYS," it's only because He loves you and has abundantly more for you than what you're experiencing.

Numbers Don't Lie

I just finished writing, "Consider Your Ways," and I thought I would follow it up with one of my favorites called, "Numbers Don't Lie." What do I mean by that?

There are so many times in our lives that we're faced with financial decisions. When we are it's always important to ask God His opinion. What would He have us do? I am a huge proponent of hearing God's voice - John 10:10: "My sheep hear my voice"- but with that being said, I know there are various ways to hear Him. Ecclesiastes 2:26 (NKJV): "For God gives wisdom and knowledge."

How does He give wisdom in financial situations?

Watch out; this is very deep: get a pencil and a piece of paper (or your computer) and start by writing down the FACTS. For example, you need a new car. Write down what you can afford right now, not what you hope to afford. Establishing an honest budget is important here, the hardest part being honest with your expenses and writing them all down.

Listen to Proverbs 4:7 (NKJV): "Wisdom is the principal thing; Therefore get wisdom. And in all your getting, get understanding." And then there is

Proverbs 19:8 (NKJV): "He who gets wisdom loves his own soul."

If we need to make a financial decision it's best to use actual numbers to assist us in seeking and knowing God's will. Continuing with the car example: I need to buy a car and have $202.00 dollars a month available to purchase it, but the car I want requires a monthly payment of $438.00. Lord, should I buy this car?

What do you believe God would say in this scenario?

To be fair, there ARE those RARE moments when God will go ahead and say "Yes, buy the car." But hear me – they are RARE.

Listen, NUMBERS DON'T LIE…

I Will Show You

You have to hear this simple yet life-changing word from the Lord. And beyond it being a word, it is a promise. If you want to see and want to know, then hear this promise: "I will show you." Revelation 4:1 (NKJV) says, "After these things I looked, and behold, a door standing open in heaven. And the first voice which I heard was like a trumpet speaking with me, saying, 'Come up here, and I will show you things which must take place after this.' "

There are some key points. First, we need to know that heaven is open 24/7. When Jesus died and the temple veil was torn from top to bottom, he made a way for all of us to have access into heaven and God's throne room.

Matthew 27:51 (NKJV): "Then, behold, the veil of the temple was torn in two from top to bottom; and the earth quaked, and the rocks were split."

Secondly, we must "leave" our natural/carnal ways/mind. We must put on the mind of Christ:

Revelation 1:10 (NKJV): "I was in the Spirit on the Lord's Day, and I heard behind me a loud voice, as of a trumpet." Before John could hear he had to be in the Spirit.

Romans 8:6-7 (NKJV): "For to be carnally minded is death, but to be spiritually minded is life and peace. Because the carnal mind is enmity against God; for it is not subject to the law of God, nor indeed can be."

And then there is 1 Corinthians 2:14 (NKJV): "But the natural man does not receive the things of the Spirit of God, for they are foolishness to him; nor can he know them, because they are spiritually discerned."

Then we read God's promise "I will show you." It doesn't say "might," it says "will."

Revelation 4:1: "Come up here, and I will show you things which must take place after this."

Psalm 2:8: "Ask me…"

Isaiah 45:11: "Ask Me of things to come concerning My sons."

I love the attitude of King Zedekiah in Jeremiah 38:14 when he says to Jeremiah, "Hide nothing from me."

Jesus speaking in Matthew 7:7-8 (NKJV):

"Ask, and it will be given to you; seek, and you will find; knock, and it will be opened to you. For everyone who asks receives, and he who seeks finds, and to him who knocks it will be opened."

Matthew 7:9 (NKJV): "Or what man is there among you who, if his son asks for bread, will give him a stone?"

Know this: our Father delights in revealing Himself to us.

John 14:21 (NKJV): "He who has My commandments and keeps them, it is he who loves Me. And he who loves Me will be loved by My Father, and I will love him and manifest Myself to him."

The final word is: HE WILL SHOW YOU…

The Absalom Spirit

The Absalom Spirit. Perhaps this is one of the most dangerous attitudes that can be in a church, a ministry, a business, and even in a home. Do you remember Absalom? He was the son of David who wanted to be king. Because of his goal he would go to the city gate early in the morning, and there he would undermine his father's authority.

By definition the Absalom Spirit is one that either knowingly or unknowingly undercuts or questions authority. It's exhibited in a person who criticizes the way things are being done. They always have a better idea, and their way is always superior. Behind your back they talk to others about you. They want change, telling others their opinion or criticizing the pastor. This "spirit" can destroy a person, pastor, church, business, family, or ministry.

Let's look at what Absalom did. "Now Absalom would rise early and stand beside the way to the gate. So it was, whenever anyone who had a lawsuit came to the king for a decision, that Absalom would call to him and say, 'What city are you from?' And he would say, 'Your servant is from such and such a tribe of Israel.' Then Absalom would say to him, 'Look, your case is good and right; but there is no deputy of the king to hear you.' Moreover, Absalom would say, 'Oh, that I were made judge in the land, and everyone who has any suit or cause would come to me; then I would give him justice.' And so it was, whenever anyone came near to bow down to him, that he would put out his hand and take him and kiss him. In this manner Absalom acted toward all Israel who came to the king for judgment. So Absalom stole the hearts of the men of Israel." (2 Samuel 15: 2-6)

An example of another person who had his own agenda is Judas. He felt that if he had Jesus arrested than Jesus would rise up and establish the Kingdom of God on earth, thus overthrowing the oppressive government/authority of the Roman government.

The result in both Judas' and Absalom's life was to create a mess that eventually got them killed.

This is true for us as well. Do you talk to others about the person/leader/pastor above you? Do you criticize them? Do you say to others, we should be doing this and that? Your intention might be to help the pastor/person by getting people to pray for them, but the overall effect is to tear apart.

Indeed the destruction that this "spirit" can unleash in a church or any other setting can be devastating. On top of that, the person being "criticized" often feels something is wrong and may feel oppressed or confused. Yes, Satan does some of his best work in this environment.

I'm not saying that we can't talk to others about people, but it's how and what we talk about, essentially the heart and attitude behind it. We're not to find fault, slander them, or gossip about them.

Absalom had a different vision than his father, and he expressed it to others and tried to get people to accept it. I call this "DI – VISION." Satan just loves division in a church, family, or business. It becomes his playground.

God Has A Rope

In Jeremiah 38 we find that King Zedikiah has given permission to four leaders of his government to throw Jeremiah into an old cistern that is empty of water but full of mud. Why? Because he doesn't like the word that Jeremiah delivered to him.

Cisterns varied in size. Likely the cistern Jeremiah was in was a common cistern thought to be 15-20 feet deep with an opening two to three feet wide. It was believed that Jeremiah was in mud that went as high as his upper thighs.

Let's read Jeremiah 38:6-13 (NKJV): "So they took Jeremiah and cast him into the dungeon of Malchiah, the king's son, which was in the court of the prison, and they let Jeremiah down with ropes. And in the dungeon there was no water, but mire. So Jeremiah sank in the mire."

Imagine what it would be like to be in mud thigh-high? Well, in a way we can, because at some point all of us have felt like we were stuck and in a dark place. At those times how often have we cried out to the Lord saying, "Lord, deliver me!"

Many times it seems that He can't hear us because we're so deep inside the cistern. Then suddenly... God has a rope to pull us out of the muck and mire.

Let's read verses 10-13: "Then the king commanded Ebed-Melech the Ethiopian, saying, 'Take from here thirty men with you, and lift Jeremiah the prophet out of the dungeon before he dies.' So Ebed-Melech took the men with him and went into the house of the king under the treasury, and took from there old clothes and old rags, and let them down by ropes into the dungeon to Jeremiah. Then Ebed-Melech the Ethiopian said to Jeremiah, 'Please put these old clothes and rags under your armpits, under the ropes.' And Jeremiah did so. So they pulled Jeremiah up with ropes and lifted him out of the dungeon. And Jeremiah remained in the court of the prison."

Did you notice that they tied together old clothes and old rags to rescue him? God has the oddest ways to pull us out of the places we're stuck in.

I want you all to know that God Has A Rope... Even when you feel it's hopeless - God Has A Rope... When you cry out, and you feel like you're not being heard - God Has A Rope... When you're discouraged and weary - God Has A Rope... When you've been misunderstood - God Has A Rope...

Not Knowing

I can hear the heart of so many of God's sons and daughters. They are crying out, "Lead me, show me!"

But when God shows us what to do, He doesn't often give us the specific details. The reason He doesn't is that if He told us everything, we would attempt to do things our own way. We would create our own plan. Another problem is our desire to be in control. We like things to go in such a way that makes us comfortable.

Wherever did we get the idea that we are the master planners?

As I'm sitting here this morning writing this, I can see a captain of an ocean liner with a bullhorn in his hand making an announcement. Can you hear what he's saying? He's telling us to "Abandon ship." It reminds me of when Paul was being taken to Rome by ship, and a fierce storm arose and the ship hit the rocks just off the island of Malta. In the middle of the raging storm the centurion who had charge of bringing Paul and the others to Rome refused to kill them. He instead instructed those who were able to jump into the raging sea and swim to the island. And those who couldn't swim he told to grab ahold of something and just hang on.

Read Acts 27:43-44 (NKJV): "But the centurion, wanting to save Paul, kept them from their purpose, and commanded that those who could swim should jump overboard first and get to land, and the rest, some on boards and some on parts of the ship. And so it was that they all escaped safely to land." The plan and instructions of the centurion were unpleasant to say the least, a plan we certainly wouldn't choose, but similar to us at times, they had no options. Here it says that they all survived.

One of my favorite verses to quote is "Abraham went out not knowing where he was going." It's from Hebrews 11:8 (NKJV): "By faith Abraham obeyed when he was called to go out to the place which he would receive as an inheritance. And he went out, not knowing where he was going."

When we read the account of Abraham we discover he didn't respond right away. It took years for him to come to a place where he trusted God to work everything out.

So be at peace knowing that God understands the process of trusting Him and letting go of control. That being said, the faster we can trust Him, the sooner we will embark on an extraordinary life.

I encourage you to be willing to respond to God even though you don't have all the facts or details. After all, you have been invited to a life of faith which is often played out in the land of not knowing. Verses like Hebrews 12:2 (NKJV): "looking unto Jesus, the author and finisher of our faith," are great, but living them out is not always easy. Ask Moses at the Red Sea and Joshua at the Jordon. And how about David when he faced Goliath?

We all want to please our Father. Extending faith is part of it. Hebrews 11:6 (NKJV): "But without faith it is impossible to please Him, for he who comes to God must believe that He is, and that He is a rewarder of those who diligently seek Him."

We are all being called to a deeper level of faith that requires "not knowing where we are going."

You Can't Have My Peace

When Jesus died he left all of us an inheritance. Ephesians 1:11 (NKJV) says, "In Him also we have obtained an inheritance."

Despite what the word says, it's taken me years to truly understand that I don't have to wait to die before I receive my inheritance. It's true that I'll receive additional inheritance after I die, but it doesn't stop me from receiving what is available now.

I came to understood something important: at the point I came to faith and was born again, I entered the Kingdom of God; I didn't need to wait until after death. John 3:5 (NKJV) says, "Jesus answered, 'Most assuredly, I say to you, unless one is born of water and the Spirit, he cannot enter the kingdom of God.' " Then in John 3:3 (NKJV): "Jesus answered and said to him, 'Most assuredly, I say to you, unless one is born again, he cannot see the kingdom of God.' " Jesus said we could both see it and enter it, and then Paul writes in Romans 14:17 (NKJV): "for the kingdom of God is not eating and drinking, but righteousness and peace and joy in the Holy Spirit."

Our Father's kingdom is not about stuff, or even eating and drinking; it's having righteousness (a right standing with God), peace (John 14:27 NKJV: "Peace I leave with you, My peace I give to you; not as the world gives do I give to you."), and joy.

Jesus makes it clear in John 10:10 that Satan came to steal, but He came to give us an abundant life. John 10:10 (NKJV): "The thief does not come except to steal, and to kill, and to destroy. I have come that they may have life, and that they may have it more abundantly." Jesus is talking about an abundant life NOW. In addition to this, Jesus is the Prince of Peace, and Jesus lives in us…

So when I realized I could have peace even in the midst of the storms of life, I determined to have that peace. We see this in Mark 4:27-40: "And a great windstorm arose, and the waves beat into the boat, so that it was already filling. But He was in the stern, asleep on a pillow. And they awoke Him and said to Him, 'Teacher, do You not care that we are perishing?' Then He arose and rebuked the wind, and said to the sea, 'Peace, be still!' And the wind ceased and there was a great calm. But He said to them, 'Why are you so fearful? How is it that you have no faith?' " In the middle of the storm Jesus has peace. He then rebukes the disciples for lacking it.

Jesus left us an inheritance of peace. Why would I allow situations and circumstances to steal it from me? Determine with me that you will declare, "You can't have my peace."

Giving Yourself Permission to Be Carnal

Many of the things I've written about in this book come from sayings that I've fashioned over the course of my walk. This is one of them.

Over and over again through the years I've seen people give themselves permission to act carnally or to live in their flesh. If you think about it, though, it's really stupid of us and simply not worth it. Ultimately, we want to be able to say of ourselves what Jesus said in John 14:7, "If you have seen me you have seen the Father."

If reflecting our Heavenly Father is our goal, then being carnal doesn't contribute in any way, nor does it give us peace...

Paul has a lot to say about living carnally:

Romans 8:5-7 (NKJV): "For those who live according to the flesh set their minds on the things of the flesh, but those who live according to the Spirit, the things of the Spirit. For to be carnally minded is death, but to be spiritually minded is life and peace. Because the carnal mind is enmity against God; for it is not subject to the law of God, nor indeed can be."

James 1:20 (NKJV): "for the wrath of man does not produce the righteousness of God," and from the (ERV) "Anger does not help you live the way God wants."

Then we have God's instruction to Moses on behalf of the children of Israel:

Deuteronomy 30:19 (NKJV): "I call heaven and earth as witnesses today against you, that I have set before you life and death, blessing and cursing; therefore choose life, that both you and your descendants may live."

It really is that simple: choose life.

What's in Your Hand?

This is the question that God asks Moses as He's recounting His plan to deliver Israel from slavery. This follows Exodus chapter three where Moses encounters God at the burning bush.

Try and picture yourself on the mountain. The bush is on fire, but it's not being consumed, and then to top it off...there's a voice coming out of the fire! It's one of those kairos moments. Kairos (καιρός) is an ancient Greek work meaning the "right or opportune moment" (the supreme moment). In the New Testament kairos means, "the appointed time in the purpose of God" which requires an action. (From Wikipedia, the free encyclopedia)

So as God is talking to Moses about him being the person He's chosen to use to deliver Israel from slavery, Moses steps back in time and recalls an earlier failure. Why does he do this? Why do any of us, for that matter, immediately go running to our data banks of the past?

Quite often it's an indicator that we're still in need of healing from our past mistakes and failures. Too often people are anchored to their past, which in turn stops them from stepping into their tomorrow.'

In this case Moses makes the comment that so many of us make when God asks us to do something. We begin focusing on our perceived abilities and in the process fail to focus on what God says He will do. We see this in Exodus 4:1 (NKJV): "Then Moses answered and said, 'But suppose they will not believe me or listen to my voice; suppose they say, "The Lord has not appeared to you." ' "

Moses was remembering 40 years previous to that when they didn't believe he'd be able to deliver them from Pharaoh. He was thinking, "Who am I and what do I have that people would follow me? What authority or power do I have?"

Watch God's response in verse 2, "So the Lord said to him, 'What is that in your hand?' He said, 'A rod.' " In our natural thinking we're looking for an answer akin to, "I will send legions of angels to fight for you, I will persuade Pharaoh to let my people go." Most of the time we're not prepared for unusual or "out-of-the-box" responses. When God asked him what was in his hand, in effect He was saying, "Use what you have."

Often when we look back at our search for something more, we find that all we ever needed was exactly what we had all along. Unto ourselves we want more anointing. God is saying, "Use the anointing you have."

This is God's message to Gideon later in the biblical account, when Israel is oppressed and outnumbered again by the Midianites. But first, Gideon, who's in hiding, says the following:

"O my lord, if the Lord is with us, why then has all this happened to us? And where are all His miracles which our fathers told us about, saying, 'Did not the Lord bring us up from Egypt?' But now the Lord has forsaken us and delivered us into the hands of the Midianites." (Judges 6:13-14 NKJV)

"Then the Lord turned to him and said, 'Go in this might of yours, and you shall save Israel from the hand of the Midianites. Have I not sent you?' "

Listen, we are the mighty men and women of God, his sons and daughters. We must stop looking at our inadequacies, our past failures, at what we don't have.

WHAT'S IN YOUR HAND?

God Will Not Forget You

Have there been times in your life when you feel like God's forgotten you?

There have been plenty for me. I've felt many times that God was not interested in me, my life, or anything that was going on in it. It seemed like He was on vacation in Bermuda and that He could care less.

If you've felt this way I want to tell you that you're not alone. Here are some thoughts from the Psalms:

Psalm 42:9 (NKJV): "I will say to God my Rock, 'Why have You forgotten me?' "

Psalm 31:12 (NKJV): "I am forgotten like a dead man, out of mind; I am like a broken vessel."

Here is our Father's response, our Abba, who does not forget His "kids:"

Isaiah 44:21 (Voice): "O Israel, remember—you are Mine. I made you; you are My servant; I will not forget you."

Abba will not forget His covenant (promises) He has made with us:

Exodus 4:5: "And I have also heard the groaning of the children of Israel whom the Egyptians keep in bondage, and I have remembered My covenant."

Abba will not forget us when our only hope is in Him:

Genesis 8:1: "Then God remembered Noah, and every living thing, and all the animals that were with him in the ark."

Abba will not forget us when our heart is broken, we feel rejected, and we wonder if He's even listening:

Genesis 30:22-23: "Then God remembered Rachel, and God listened to her and opened her womb. And she conceived and bore a son, and said, 'God has taken away my reproach.' "

Abba also remembered Hannah, rejected and despised because she was barren. God gave her a son:

1 Samuel 1:19: "And Elkanah knew Hannah his wife, and the Lord remembered her."

God will not forget you…

I Don't Know What to Say

I can't begin to tell you how often I've heard people say to me:

"I can't talk to people about God because I don't know what to say."

"I am lost for words."

"I'm not very good at speaking."

They're not alone. There are times before pastors' conferences when I feel inadequate. I ask myself "Who am I?" Then the belief surfaces that I'm not a good speaker - and all this from one who's been preaching for 67 years. It's real that between my natural mind and the devil there's a plan to silence me, and it's true for you too.

Moses felt inadequate. In Exodus chapter four when God gives him instruction about how to use the rod in his hand, Moses responds: "I have never been a good speaker. I wasn't one before you spoke to me, and I'm not one now. I am slow at speaking, and I can never think of what to say." (Exodus 4:10)

God's response to Moses is beautiful, one He's also speaking to us. He will teach us. "So the Lord said to him, 'Who has made man's mouth? Or who makes the mute, the deaf, the seeing, or the blind? Have not I, the Lord? Now therefore, go, and I will be with your mouth and teach you what you shall say.' " (Exodus 4: 10-11)

God tells us that He's delivered us and He will work in us. Psalm 81:10 (NKJV) says, "I am the Lord your God, Who brought you out of the land of Egypt; Open your mouth wide, and I will fill it."

Our problem is that we look at our abilities and not the enabling power of God to fulfill what He has PROMISED. It's believed by many that the Apostle Paul stuttered when he spoke, which is perhaps why he wrote, "I was with you in weakness, in fear, and in much trembling" (1 Corinthians 2:3, NKJV) and other confessional-type statements he shared about his life.

Then there is Philippians 4:13 (NKJV): "I can do all things through Christ who strengthens me." The Greek says, "what he retires of me" and the Amplified says, "I can do all things [which He has called me to do] through Him who strengthens and empowers me [to fulfill His purpose—I am self-sufficient in Christ's sufficiency; I am ready for anything and equal to anything through Him who infuses me with inner strength and confident peace.]"

Let's make up our minds that we won't be silenced any more. Instead, we'll declare what God has spoken – "Open your mouth wide, and I will fill it."

Mental Gymnastics

Mental gymnastics is the practice of spending minutes, hours, and even days repeatedly thinking, contemplating, and pondering something in our minds without having all the facts.

When we're in the position of being ignorant of all the details, we draw conclusions and imagine scenarios that don't exist. We try our hardest to guess every why and because. Why did they do this, why did they do that? We presume to know what people are thinking and feeling and in the process, end up judging their heart. Unfortunately, once we do this we often begin treating that person differently or at best awkwardly because we've more than likely made wrong assumptions.

We can also exercise (appropriate term, because it's exhausting) premature judgment in regard to situations and circumstances. Just say for an example we want to buy a home and so put a bid in on it. When we don't hear back for two days, we think and think and draw this and that conclusion. Then we find out that the realtor was sick or an emergency came up in his or her life, or maybe that the buyer (who's doing their own mental gymnastics) never received our offer.

Our assuming and presuming will lead us to various beliefs, actions, and consequences:

Proverbs 23:7 (NKJV): "For as he thinks in his heart, so is he."

James 1:8 (NKJV): "a double-minded man, unstable in all his ways"

1 Kings 18:21 (NKJV): "And Elijah came to all the people, and said, 'How long will you falter between two opinions?' "

Romans 14:4 (NKJV): "Who are you to judge another's servant?"

Look at what happens to us when we engage in mental gymnastics. It's clearly not worth it.

Is there a way we can avoid this futility?

Thankfully, yes! In Isaiah 26:3 (NKJV) it says, "You will keep him in perfect peace, Whose mind is stayed on You, Because he trusts in You."

You Have to Be Flexible

I think by now we've all learned that to think and live within the natural and logical borders of life is to restrict and limit God. It's summed up by the expression, "If you don't bend, you'll break."

Being flexible doesn't mean compromising the word of God, but it does mean being open to allowing the Holy Spirit, within the boundaries of scripture, to do things another way. To be honest, sometimes we can over-spiritualize things. Sometimes we equate personal preferences to the way God wants us to do things. But in reality, our "way" can often be nothing more than our own stubbornness or insistence on what we want.

There are times when we run into spiritual detours. This means we want to go in a certain direction, but the Holy Spirit has another way of getting us there. I'm recalling Peter in the book of Acts. He has his theology, his way of doing things, the ways he feels comfortable and fully persuaded, yet God shows up messing with all of it. Peter was a Jew and had never eaten "unclean" food. While he's lived this way his entire life, God comes to show him something new.

We read in Acts 10:13-16: "And a voice came to him, 'Rise, Peter; kill and eat.' But Peter said, 'Not so, Lord! For I have never eaten anything common or unclean.' And a voice spoke to him again the second time, 'What God has cleansed you must not call common.' This was done three times. And the object was taken up into heaven again."

Notice that it took three times before Peter was willing to see things differently. The question is: are we willing to see things differently? Or will the habits and even ruts in our lives cause us to miss out on what God wants to do in the moment?

The following two verses have literally changed my life:

1 Samuel 10:7 (NKJV): "And let it be, when these signs come to you, that you do as the occasion demands; for God is with you."

Yes, through God we're able to discern what to do in any given moment, not what we did yesterday or at another time in our life, but what we're going to do in that very minute and circumstance. You see Peter would never have gone to minister at the house of Cornelius. But after God speaks to him three times, he is finally willing to yield to a new way. I wonder what God's alternative plan would have been if Peter hadn't been flexible?

I'm always grateful that our God continues to reach out to us, showing us another way, a concept applied as much to the small matters and details in life as to the large.

The second verse that's been powerful to me is John 3:8 (NKJV):

"The wind blows where it wishes, and you hear the sound of it, but cannot tell where it comes from and where it goes. So is everyone who is born of the Spirit."

This catching or discerning the wind is important in sailing too; without it, no one would move. Heavy winds require certain sails, while lighter winds require different ones, and if the wind is not blowing at all, then it's necessary to use the engine.

So it is with us. Learning to discern the "wind" of God is critical.

In the hundreds of meetings I've attended, I've often had a particular idea of what I've wanted to see done or accomplished. Yet I have to be flexible and willing to yield to what the Holy Spirit wants to do, not what I want to do. Just recently I was on a trip and before the service felt that the Holy Spirit wanted me to go in a certain direction. As the meeting progressed, however, it was clear that God had something else in mind. So instead of me doing what I'd wanted, I happily responded to the new direction, and God ended up moving in a powerful way.

The principle of remaining flexible can be uncomfortable at times, but we need to ask ourselves what we'd rather do - live in our comfort or in what the Holy Spirit wants to do in the moment.

We have to be flexible...

Who Told You?

The second question God asked Adam is found in Genesis 3:11 (NKJV): "Who told you...?"

This is a question I ask myself a lot, and you might consider asking yourself the same. You see, many times thoughts come streaming into our minds, and too often we attribute them to ourselves, but in reality they're coming from the enemy of our souls.

Have you had thoughts about being inferior to people around you? That you're not important and nobody will miss you? You don't belong? Someone else can do a better job than you? Nobody listens to you so why bother saying anything? Whatever spiritual gift you have doesn't compare to someone else's gift? You don't sing very well? You don't teach very well? You don't prophesy very well so why even bother using your gift at all? In fact, why even bother going to church? Oh, and that you don't need to tithe? In fact, you should keep your money and buy that thing you've always wanted? You can give next week if you can afford it? They're asking for help but you're too busy? Oh, and did you notice that Pastor So and So didn't say hello to you today? And his wife never came over to you, but look who she's talking to now?

Paul gives us great counsel in 2 Corinthians 10:4-5 (NKJV) where he writes, "For the weapons of our warfare are not carnal but mighty in God for pulling down strongholds, casting down arguments and every high thing that exalts itself against the knowledge of God, bringing every thought into captivity to the obedience of Christ."

Now Paul wouldn't write something from the Holy Spirit that we aren't capable of doing. We can take every thought captive… We can!

I'm Not Interested in Your Opinion

When you're looking to make a major decision, watch out for whose opinions you gather. In reality, you're not looking for someone else's opinion, and furthermore, shouldn't even be interested in your own. Remember Proverbs 14:12 and 16:25 where it says in the New King James Version, "There is a way that seems right to a man, but it's end is the way of death."

We don't need thoughts and opinions that only seem right to us. If we're honest, we're all pretty aware when we're hearing what we want to. It's called "selective hearing."

But think about it; do you want God's opinion or your own?

In 1 Kings 22 Ahab is trying to persuade Jehoshaphat to go to war with him against Syria and gathers his false prophets to ask their advice. 1 Kings 22:6 (NKJV): "Then the king of Israel gathered the prophets together, about four hundred men, and said to them, 'Shall I go against Ramoth Gilead to fight, or shall I refrain?' So they said, 'Go up, for the Lord will deliver it into the hand of the king.' "

Jehoshaphat hears what they say but isn't interested in it so asks again. (1 Kings 22:7): "And Jehoshaphat said, 'Is there not still a prophet of the Lord here, that we may inquire of Him?' "

Watch King Ahab's response to Jehoshaphat. It's very interesting and may even reflect our own attitude at times. (Verse 8): "So the king of Israel said to Jehoshaphat, 'There is still one man, Micaiah the son of Imlah, by whom we may inquire of the Lord; but I hate him, because he does not prophesy good concerning me, but evil.' And Jehoshaphat said, 'Let not the king say such things!' (verse 9) "Then the king of Israel called an officer and said, 'Bring Micaiah the son of Imlah quickly!' "

So Micaiah shows up and in verse 14 says (and I'm paraphrasing): "I'm here not to give my opinion or the opinion of others." Listen to his words from 1 Kings 22:14 (NKJV): "As the Lord lives, whatever the Lord says to me, that I will speak."

Micaiah is not interested in offering his opinions, suggestions, or thoughts. He had a responsibility - as do we - to report what God says.

We don't need opinions. We need a word from the Lord.

Help Me Understand

This short phrase has been such a blessing to me and quite frankly, has kept me from saying things I shouldn't.

During innumerable times of conflict someone does something to anger me, and in the moment it's impossible to comprehend what they've done or said. Those are the times that tend to either stir existing negative emotions or birth new ones. And through it all, yes… I've wanted to strangle people, tell them off, and a bunch of other things.

In the early 1980s I began my role as the primary counselor in our church. I would spend hours and hours listening to people and heard things which caused my mind and emotions to travel in diverse directions. And then came the expectation of my providing input.

The first thing I came to see in myself was the need to have a right heart. I could give input, but it's how I gave it that mattered. I might have had the right council but the wrong heart, and people could always tell the difference.

Here I was, sitting for hours giving counsel, but needing to know the right way to express it. How could I say things in such a way that wouldn't hurt, offend, or alienate them? Then one day, the answer came - say to them – "Help me understand…"

Then all these verses came alive to me and became very practical:

Proverbs 4:5 (NKJV): "Get wisdom! Get understanding!"

Proverbs 4:7 (NKJV): "Wisdom is the principal thing; Therefore get wisdom. And in all your getting, get understanding."

Proverbs 18:13 (NKJV): "He who answers a matter before he hears it, It is folly and shame to him." The Message Bible: "Answering before listening is both stupid and rude."

Proverbs 20:3 (NKJV): "It is honorable for a man to stop striving, Since any fool can start a quarrel."

Romans 12:18 (NKJV): "If it is possible, as much as depends on you, live peaceably with all men."

I needed to be part of the solution. I needed in many cases, to defuse impending disaster. Save marriages. Pull people out from financial disaster. Yet sadly, in the midst of listening I would often sit there and think, "Boy have they made some stupid decisions!"

That's when I knew I had to change. I needed to have what Galatians 5:6 calls, "faith working through love." I needed to know why. Why and how did they get to these points? While I might not have had the answer they needed or even wanted to hear, I needed to communicate to them that they were loved.

So when a situation arises with your mate, your small children, teenagers, friends, or anyone else - particularly one which might cause you to react - stop and offer this three-word response:

Help me understand....

Developing A God-Consciousness

Omnipresent is a theological term which means that God is present everywhere at the same time. God is here with me in Rehoboth, Massachusetts, and God is with all the people and pastors I know all over the world at the very same moment in time.

The amazing thing is that while we say it, we really don't believe it. In most of our church services we pray and ask the Holy Spirit to come, yet why do we need to if He's already there? Especially during times of turmoil or difficulty we tend to ask God where He is.

His Answer? I am right here with you. Four times in Genesis chapter 39, in fact, it says, "The Lord was with Joseph."

Genesis 39: 2, 3, 21, 23 (NKJV):

2 - "The Lord was with Joseph, and he was a successful man; and he was in the house of his master the Egyptian." (after he was sold into slavery)

3 - "And his master saw that the Lord was with him and that the Lord made all he did [a]to prosper in his hand."

21 - "But the Lord was with Joseph and showed him mercy, and He gave[a] him favor in the sight of the keeper of the prison." (after he was falsely accused of adultery)

23 - "The keeper of the prison did not look into anything that was under Joseph's authority, because the Lord was with him; and whatever he did, the Lord made it prosper."

We must begin seizing the reality that God is always with us and in us. The example I always point to is from Genesis 28:10-12 & 16 (NKJV):

"Now Jacob went out from Beersheba and went toward Haran. So he came to a certain place and stayed there all night, because the sun had set. And he took one of the stones of that place and put it at his head, and he lay down in that place to sleep. Then he dreamed, and behold, a ladder was set up on the earth, and its top reached to heaven; and there the angels of God were ascending and descending on it. Then Jacob awoke from his sleep and said, 'Surely the Lord is in this place, and I did not know it.' "

The next verse says that Jacob built an altar because he wanted to worship and secondly, he wanted to remember. Yes, two things the presence of God should provoke us to do are: worship and build an altar (or place in our hearts), not forgetting how God literally meets with us, and even when we don't feel it or perceive it, is always present.

When you begin developing a God-Consciousness you will be shocked how often you'll sense the omnipresence of God in your everyday life…

Tipping or Tithing

I want to express my profound sadness over a major change I've seen in the church since 1970. It concerns tithing.

When I became a son of God in 1970, tithing was an absolute conviction in the majority of evangelical, charismatic, and pentecostal churches. It's not exaggeration to say that it was enthusiastically embraced by people and went far beyond obligation to giving with a true sense of joy.

Embracing the principle in Deuteronomy meant arriving at church on Sunday with tithes and yes, even offerings above our tithe. Though the scripture speaks specifically about the Holy Days, we can't miss the principle:

"Three times a year all your males shall appear before the Lord your God in the place which He chooses: at the Feast of Unleavened Bread, at the Feast of Weeks, and at the Feast of Tabernacles; and they shall not appear before the Lord empty-handed." (Deuteronomy 16:16, NKJV)

Throughout the church I hear the belief that tithing is under the law, and because of that people don't need to practice it. True, you don't have to tithe, but choosing whether or not to tithe is an issue of the heart. This principle is in Luke 12:34 and Matthew 6:21 (NKJV): "For where your treasure is, there your heart will be also."

All money, in fact everything, belongs to God:

1 Corinthians 10:26 (NKJV): "the earth is the Lord's, and all its fullness."

Haggai 2:8 (NKJV): " 'The silver is Mine, and the gold is Mine,' says the Lord of hosts."

Abraham tithed to Melchizedek before the advent of the law. It seems clear enough in the Genesis 14:20 account that for Abraham, paying the tithe to Melchizedek was an act of worship.

Hebrews 7: 1-3 (NKJV): "For this Melchizedek, king of Salem, priest of the Most High God, who met Abraham returning from the slaughter of the kings and blessed him, to whom also Abraham gave a tenth part of all, first being translated 'king of righteousness,' and then also king of Salem, meaning 'king of peace,' without father, without mother, without genealogy, having neither beginning of days nor end of life, but made like the Son of God, remains a priest continually."

Jacob also vows to tithe, and this too is before the time of the law:

Genesis 28:20-22: "Then Jacob made a vow, saying, 'I God will be with me, and keep me in this way that I am going, and give me bread to eat and clothing to put on, so that I come back to my father's house in peace, then the Lord shall be my God. And this stone which I have set as a pillar shall be God's house, and of all that You give me I will surely give a tenth to You.' "

Malachi's big question and conclusion:

Malachi 3:8 (NKJV): "Will a man rob God? Yet you have robbed Me! But you say, 'In what way have we robbed You? In tithes and offerings.' "

Malachi 3:10 (NKJV): "'Bring all the tithes into the storehouse, That there may be food in My house, 'And try Me now in this,' says the Lord of hosts, 'If I will not open for you the windows of heaven And pour out for you such blessing That there will not be room enough to receive it.' "

Though many can't realistically give ten percent of their income, some lesser portion set aside and given faithfully meets the heart of the Father. Then you'll see blessings come in several different ways, not just in money. We had a set of tires, for example, last 99,000 miles. Also, when our car wouldn't run we laid hands on it and it ran (this happened several times); the same thing happened to our dryer. After some time you might hear God ask whether you can afford x dollars more. And at that point you'll say, "Sure."

If we want to be honest, how much money do we spend on coffee, donuts, fast food, pizza, and similar things? Perhaps this is something to consider.

There are two verses in 2 Corinthians that talk about God loving a cheerful giver, and while it's true that they're in direct reference to giving for missions, the overall principle is important:

2 Corinthians 9: 6-7: "But this I say: He who sows sparingly will also reap sparingly, and he who sows [c]bountifully will also reap bountifully. So let each one give as he purposes in his heart, not grudgingly or of necessity; for God loves a cheerful giver."

Tithing is not a law but rather, a principle akin to gravity. It works like gravity, but the natural eye doesn't see it.

Tipping or tithing? We can give God a gift of money based on what we want to give rather than on the clear principle of giving the 10% tithe. This is more like tipping. Money we're led to give unrelated to our tithe is called an offering. Offerings are wonderful but should not replace our tithe.

My Joy is You

On the outside I'm not that emotional; nevertheless my whole being burns with a passion to see each and every son and daughter of God become all that they're created to be.

I so desire people to know God and to walk in His presence on a daily basis, with the final goal of being in His presence forever.

1 Thessalonians 2 :19 (NKJV) "For what is our hope, or joy, or crown of rejoicing? Is it not even you in the presence of our Lord Jesus Christ at His coming?"

Yes, you are my joy and crown of rejoicing. This is one of the reasons I'm writing this book. My heart-cry is, "Lord whatever I can do to see people know you and your presence and the power of God in them, I will do."

When I see people walking in everything that God has created them to be, it's such an overwhelming joy. The Apostle John expresses this in 3 John 1:4:

"I have no greater joy than to hear that my children walk in truth."

I continually cry out that each one of you would know Him and the power of His resurrection, to really know Him intimately and to know the power of God that is in you.

Philippians 3:10 (NKJV): "...that I may know Him and the power of His resurrection..."

The verse continues on to say that Paul is willing to be identified with Christ even if it includes hardship and difficulties, willing to give everything, even his life.

Verse 10: "...and the fellowship of His sufferings, being conformed to His death..."

John 15:13 (NKJV): "Greater love has no one than this, than to lay down one's life for his friends."

There is a call for us to walk in the footsteps of Jesus.

1 Peter 2:21 (NKJV): "For to this you were called, because Christ also suffered for us, leaving us an example, that you should follow His steps."

Perhaps you are the only Jesus that people might see or encounter. And yes, it might come at a cost. Paul puts it this way:

Philippians 2:17 (NKJV): "Yes, and if I am being poured out as a drink offering on the sacrifice and service of your faith, I am glad and rejoice with you all."

2 Timothy 4:6 (NKJV): "For I am already being poured out as a drink offering…"

You Have an Anointing

For too many years the church taught that only a certain few people carried an anointing. We identified the anointing to be on the pastor, perhaps too on his wife or other pastors in the church, on an elder and more often than not, to a degree, on the worship leader. We had the "haves and the have-nots."

Creating this distinction led to a failure to teach the true identity and authority of each believer. It's only been in recent years that this has changed:

1 John 2:20 (NKJV): "But you have an anointing from the Holy One."

John was writing this to the entire church, to everyone, not just to a select few. All too often people look at others who are walking in their anointing and compare themselves. John was saying that everyone has an anointing.

Paul, on the other hand, is clear about there being different degrees of a gifting.

Romans 12:3 (NKJV): "For I say, through the grace given to me, to everyone who is among you, not to think of himself more highly than he ought to think but to think soberly, as God has dealt to each one a measure of faith."

Jesus sent out the 12 disciples:

Luke 9:1-2 (NKJV): "Then He called His twelve disciples together and gave them power and authority over all demons, and to cure diseases. He sent them to preach the kingdom of God and to heal the sick."

He sent out the seventy disciples:

Luke 10:8-9 (NKJV): "Whatever city you enter, and they receive you, eat such things as are set before you. And heal the sick there, and say to them, 'The kingdom of God has come near to you.' "

Now he gives that charge to all of us:

Mark 16:15-18: "And He said to them, 'Go into all the world and preach the gospel to every creature. He who believes and is baptized will be saved; but he who does not believe will be condemned. And these signs will follow those who believe: In My name they will cast out demons; they will speak with new tongues; they will take up serpents; and if they drink anything deadly, it will by no means hurt them; they will lay hands on the sick, and they will recover.' "

There's no need to pray for or ask for an anointing! Just use the one you have. The more you exercise or practice your anointing, the stronger it gets. Don't be deceived any longer. Our Father didn't give to some and not to others.

It's true that He's anointed some with a greater measure of faith and of grace, but even still, do not minimize your anointing. Remember that "anointing" means "CHOSEN ONE" which applies to each and every one of us.

And is this anointing temporary or fleeting? The apostle John would say no. "But the anointing which you have received from Him abides in you." (1 John 2:27 NKJV)

No, your anointing doesn't come and go but instead, abides in you.

LISTEN: YOU HAVE AN ANOINTING…

The Issue is Not the Issue

When a problem arises we often make the mistake of not getting to its root. We misidentify the real issue or problem and end up dealing with secondary issues, thus never addressing the core problem.

When a person is angry, for example, most of the time we try and deal just with that. We are told by psychologists, however, that anger is usually not the primary issue, but rather the manifestation of deeper emotions. What's at the core is usually hurt or disappointment laid down in specific memories much earlier in the person's life.

If you picture a fruit tree and then go and pick all the fruit off the branches, in a short while, what happens? More fruit appears on the tree. Over and over we deal with anger, but it's seldom the root problem.

Perhaps an illustration would be beneficial. If you remember, in Matthew 21 Jesus sees a fig tree and when he draws close to it notices that it has lots of leaves but no fruit. There are times when plants that are supposed to flower don't, and when this happens typically the plant continues to be flowerless. You might get one flower but that's it.

If we don't deal with the root, the problem will continue to manifest, and the result will be a perpetual lack of fruit. Here is Matthew's account:

Matthew 21:19 (NKJV): "And seeing a fig tree by the road, He came to it and found nothing on it but leaves, and said to it, 'Let no fruit grow on you ever again.' Immediately the fig tree withered away."

It often takes courage to be honest and deal with the real issue. An example - when a person is demonized. You can rebuke the demon and tell it to leave, but if the source and reason it came into a person's life persists, it will keep on coming back. We need to find the open door (the reason) and then close it so the demon no longer has access. For example, holding unforgiveness can lead to what the scripture describes as torment. Harassment by a spirit therefore points to a need to uncover the root.

Let's read the parable of the unforgiving servant:

Matthew 18:28-35: "But that servant went out and found one of his fellow servants who owed him a hundred denarii; and he laid hands on him and took him by the throat, saying, 'Pay me what you owe!' So his fellow servant fell down [e]at his feet and begged him, saying, 'Have patience with me, and I will pay you [f]all.' And he would not, but went and threw him into prison till he should pay the debt. So when his fellow servants saw what had been done, they were very grieved, and came and told their master all that had been done. Then his master, after he had called him, said to him, 'You wicked servant! I forgave you all that debt because you begged me. Should you not also have had compassion on your fellow servant, just as I had pity on you?' And his master was angry, and delivered him to the torturers until he should pay all that was due to him. So My heavenly Father also will do to you if each of you, from his heart, does not forgive his brother his trespasses."

Once we get to the root of unforgiveness and deal with it, our torment will end...

Get to the root...

What if We Had Unity

In Genesis 11 we have an unbelievable story of unity. I often ponder this story, asking myself what it would be like if the church was truly unified, I mean really unified, beyond just saying it, beyond just the surface. As I read Psalm 133 I see God declaring that where there is unity, He'll command forth a blessing.

Can you dream with me about what could happen?!

Psalm 133:1-3 (NKJV): "Behold, how good and how pleasant it is For brethren to dwell together in unity! It is like the precious oil upon the head, Running down on the beard, The beard of Aaron, Running down on the edge of his garments. It is like the dew of Hermon, Descending upon the mountains of Zion; For there the Lord commanded the blessing — Life forevermore."

Here is Genesis 11:1-6 (NKJV):

"Now the whole earth had one language and one [a]speech. And it came to pass, as they journeyed from the east, that they found a plain in the land of Shinar, and they dwelt there. Then they said to one another, 'Come, let us make bricks and bake them thoroughly.' They had brick for stone, and they had asphalt for mortar. And they said, 'Come, let us build ourselves a city, and a tower whose top is in the heavens; let us make a name for ourselves, lest we be scattered abroad over the face of the whole earth.' But the Lord came down to see the city and the tower which the sons of men had built. And the Lord said, 'Indeed the people are one and they all have one language, and this is what they begin to do; now nothing that they propose to do will be withheld from them.'"

Did you see this - "Indeed the people are one and they all have one language, and this is what they begin to do; now nothing that they propose to do will be withheld from them."

I see the prayer of Jesus in John 17 still unfulfilled:

"I do not pray for these alone, but also for those who will believe in Me through their word; that they all may be one, as You, Father, are in Me, and I in You; that they also may be one in Us, that the world may believe that You sent Me." (John 17: 20-21)

Let's take a look in scripture at what happened when people were unified. In the dedicating of Solomon's Temple:

2 Chronicles 5:13-14 (NKJV): "Indeed it came to pass, when the trumpeters and singers were as one, to make one sound to be heard in praising and thanking the Lord, and when they lifted up their voice with the trumpets and cymbals and instruments of music, and praised the Lord, saying: 'For He is good, For His mercy endures forever,' that the house, the house of the Lord, was filled with a cloud, so that the priests could not continue ministering because of the cloud; for the glory of the Lord filled the house of God."

When they were in one accord in the upper room:

Acts 2:1-3 (NKJV): "When the Day of Pentecost had fully come, they were all with one accord in one place. And suddenly there came a sound from heaven, as of a rushing mighty wind, and it filled the whole house where they were sitting. Then there appeared to them divided tongues, as of fire, and one sat upon each of them."

The Apostles gather for prayer after Peter and John are released from prison:

Acts 4:23-24 & 31 (NKJV): "And being let go, they went to their own companions and reported all that the chief priests and elders had said to them. So when they heard that, they raised their voice to God with one accord.

And when they had prayed, the place where they were assembled together was shaken; and they were all filled with the Holy Spirit, and they spoke the word of God with boldness."

And lastly when they were in one accord on Solomon's Porch:

Acts 5:12 (NKJV): "And through the hands of the apostles many signs and wonders were done among the people. And they were all with one accord in Solomon's Porch."

You might think it impossible, but in my book Divine Encounters I write about what happened when we had unity. On two occasions it rained inside our church and in a high school, and a cloud also filled our sanctuary. The fire department came, and the next day a contractor, all witnessing the effect of our one accord.

WHAT IF WE REALLY HAD UNITY...

They Had Been with Jesus

In Acts chapter four we find the story of Peter and John's arrest after healing the lame man at the Gate of Beautiful. After they're taken away they're interrogated all night by the Sadducees and the next day by the Sanhedrin. When they finish, their accusers draw an amazing conclusion, one which all of us would love to be said about us. "Now when they saw the boldness of Peter and John, and perceived that they were uneducated and untrained men, they marveled. And they realized that they had been with Jesus." (Acts 4:13)

When I read this account, it causes me to ask who we've been hanging out with. After all, a person who's been around fire will naturally smell like smoke.

The more time we spend with the Trinity the more we should be reflecting the heart and character of the Father, the Son, and the Holy Spirit.

If You Have Seen Me, You Have Seen the Father

After spending time outside on a beautiful day, people will often notice and comment later, "You've been in the sun." They recognize this truth without your saying a word.

This is true of more than our physical being, and I really believe we're not fully aware of the extent of it, how very many people are watching us. They're looking to see if our faith translates to everyday life. Three times in the gospels we see Jesus make this remark:

Luke 5:20 (NKJV) "When He saw their faith…"

Our faith is tangible, on display for everyone to see. How you and I live our lives is therefore critical to the preaching of the Gospel. A quote that has been attributed to St. Francis of Assisi (though he never actually said it) is, "Always preach the gospel, and sometimes use words." Such a powerful statement.

Paul writes:

Hebrews 12:1 (NKJV): "Therefore we also, since we are surrounded by so great a cloud of witnesses, let us lay aside every weight, and the sin which so easily ensnares us, and let us run with endurance the race that is set before us."

And then we have these words of Jesus to Phillip:

John 14:9 (NKJV): "Jesus said to him, 'Have I been with you so long, and yet you have not known Me, Philip? He who has seen Me has seen the Father; so how can you say, 'Show us the Father?' "

Isn't it one of our goals that when people see us they get a glimpse of our heavenly Father? Afterall, when people look at us they're usually able to see characteristics of our earthly fathers. So should it be that they see the heavenly one.

THEY HAVE SEEN THE FATHER...

Digging New Wells

For perhaps the past 15 years or so there's been a movement within pentecostal and charismatic churches to try and rekindle the past moves of the Holy Spirit. People refer to Isaac and how he re-dug the wells of his father Abraham so the people of God could have fresh water.

Genesis 26:18: "And Isaac dug again the wells of water which they had dug in the days of Abraham his father, for the Philistines had stopped them up after the death of Abraham. He called them by the names which his father had called them."

Did you notice that the Philistines had stopped up the wells? They did this by throwing in dead animals. While I can appreciate desiring revival, I'm not interested in duplicating former ones. Praise God for what he did then, but I am looking for what He wants to do now.

Isaiah 43:18-19 (NKJV): "Do not remember the former things, Nor consider the things of old. Behold, I will do a new thing, Now it shall spring forth; Shall you not know it? I will even make a road in the wilderness And rivers in the desert."

It says not to remember or even consider the former things. But look, God wants to do a new thing... Yes, he'll make a road in the wilderness and rivers in the desert. My heart's cry - SIGN ME UP!

Jesus said that you can't put new wine in an old wine skin:

Mark 2:22 (NKJV): "And no one puts new wine into old wineskins; or else the new wine bursts the wineskins, the wine is spilled, and the wineskins are ruined. But new wine must be put into new wineskins."

Matthew 9:16 (NKJV): "No one puts a piece of unshrunk cloth on an old garment; for the patch pulls away from the garment, and the tear is made worse."

By all means thank God for everything He has done, but look also for what He wants to do TODAY...

PERHAPS YOU WOULD CONSIDER DIGGING NEW WELLS...

Where is the Power of God?

There are multiple answers, but if I may give a synopsis of why I believe we're not seeing the power of God in our churches today...

Let me begin by providing a context: the time period between the 1970s and 90s when we saw God moving in powerful ways, but... where there were some serious shortcomings:

1. We lacked the character we needed. We were much like Samson who had the anointing but lacked the necessary character - pride in particular was a huge issue.

2. We failed to teach the word of God in a consistent and contextual way. Because pastors wanted to justify certain aspects of what they claimed was God working, they would take scriptures out of context. For example, people were allowed to roar like lions during a church service, and the following verse was used to justify what was happening.

Hosea 11:10 (NKJV): "They shall walk after the Lord. He will roar like a lion. When He roars, Then His sons shall come trembling from the west."

This second verse will make you wonder who exactly was doing the roaring:

1 Peter 5:8 (NKJV): "Be sober, be vigilant; because your adversary the devil walks about like a roaring lion, seeking whom he may devour."

3. We lacked order. I don't mind laughing, crying, sobbing, and other human emotions as long as they are expressed, as Paul writes, "decently and in order." This was another weakness during this time period - a lack of pastoring the flow of the meeting. It lacked order.

1 Corinthians 14:40 (NKJV): "Let all things be done decently and in order."

Ephesians 4:14 (NKJV): "...that we should no longer be children, tossed to and fro and carried about with every wind of doctrine, by the trickery of men, in the cunning craftiness of deceitful plotting..."

In order to bring an adjustment to some of the imbalances of this time, the pendulum swung in the opposite direction. The effect was that:

4. We replaced the power of God with intellectualism, forgetting:

1 Corinthians 4:20 (NKJV): "... the kingdom of God is not in word but in power."

1 Corinthians 2:4-5 (NKJV): "And my speech and my preaching were not with persuasive words of human wisdom, but in demonstration of the Spirit and of power that your faith should not be in the wisdom of men but in the power of God."

The result of all these things is that for the past 20-25 years we have raised up a generation that has not seen the power of God. In many cases they don't want it. They are afraid of it, bringing intellect in as a most unworthy replacement. The verses in Judges chapter two apply here - after Joshua and all the elders died, another generation arose that didn't know the power of God:

Judges 2:7-10: "So the people served the Lord all the days of Joshua, and all the days of the elders who outlived Joshua, who had seen all the great works of the Lord which He had done for Israel. Now Joshua the son of Nun, the servant of the Lord, died when he was one hundred and ten years old. And they buried him within the border of his inheritance at Timnath Heres, in the mountains of Ephraim, on the north side of Mount Gaash. When all that generation had been gathered to their fathers, another generation arose after them who did not know the Lord nor the work which He had done for Israel."

I am looking for a move of God that Revelation 22 defines as a" pure river," originating from the very throne of God.

Revelation 22 (NKJV): "And he showed me a pure river of water of life, clear as crystal, proceeding from the throne of God and of the Lamb. In the middle of its street, and on either side of the river, was the tree of life, which bore twelve fruits, each tree yielding its fruit every month. The leaves of the tree were for the healing of the nations."

Father, send your power and help us learn from the past. Help us live out 2 Corinthians 4:7: "But we have this treasure in earthen vessels, that the excellence of the power may be of God and not of us." (NKJV)

You Are Going to Have to Wrestle

Did you know that God is assembling a wrestling team?

This team is comprised of people who want to have a divine encounter with God. They want to see Him and know Him face to face. They want to be changed into another man or woman and thereby permanently affected by the power and presence of God.

Listen, this is not an easy thing. It takes everything you have. When you wish it was over, it isn't. When you want to quit because it hurts, you can't. You'll discover that as in wrestling, there are moves by your opponent that surprise you and seem not only illegal, but unnecessary.

This wrestling match lasts a long time. In fact, you'll find that there are several matches you'll be involved in where you don't really want to participate. But each wrestling match is different. It will produce different results but with each, you'll know God better. You'll better understand His ways; you'll fall more and more in love with Him. Ultimately each one always brings you to a place of rejoicing.

This concept is found in Genesis 32:22-31:

"And he arose that night and took his two wives, his two female servants, and his eleven sons, and crossed over the ford of Jabbok. He took them, sent them over the brook, and sent over what he had. Then Jacob was left alone; and a Man wrestled with him until the breaking of day. Now when He saw that He did not prevail against him, He touched the socket of his hip; and the socket of Jacob's hip was out of joint as He wrestled with him. And he said, 'Let Me go, for the day breaks.' But he said, 'I will not let You go unless You bless me!' So He said to him, 'What is your name?' He said, 'Jacob.' And He said, 'Your name shall no longer be called Jacob, but Israel; for you have struggled with God and with men, and have prevailed.' Then Jacob asked, saying, 'Tell me Your name, I pray.' And He said, 'Why is it that you ask about My name?' And He blessed him there. So Jacob called the name of the place Peniel: 'For I have seen God face to face, and my life is preserved.' Just as he crossed over Peniel the sun rose on him, and he limped on his hip."

Did you notice that Jacob was left alone? It's true. A time of wrestling is usually your time with God and no one else's. Having said that, there ARE times when God wrestles with the whole team because He wants to affect overall change. Matches within marriages, families, and churches are a good example.

I just heard the referee blow his whistle indicating that the match is about to begin!

Leaving the Outer Court

The temple in Jerusalem had three distinct areas. One was the outer court where people would congregate to do their business transactions, the inner court where the priest would carry out his various daily responsibilities, and the Holy of Holies which contained the very real and tangible presence of God. The priest would only visit the latter once a year.

To me the temple exemplifies a perfect picture of worship: three different locations to praise the Lord.

The outer courts are our praise and thanksgiving music - lively and stimulating to our soul.

The inner court is our quiet place where we sing or play music which causes us to be reflective

The Holy of Holies is the place of intimacy. It's where we worship God for who He is and what He's done for us. It's the place we literally encounter the living God, the place where we're overwhelmed by His love and affection and where His voice becomes clear and distinct.

I am faced with the question of why I would want to spend any time in the outer or inner courts when I can bypass them both and find myself in the Holy of Holies?

Can we leave the outer courts to pursue the place where we divinely encounter God, a place that beckons us to come, where we join the living creatures, the 24 elders, and the angels of heaven?

Can you hear the call from Revelation 4:1: "After these things I looked, and behold, a door standing open in heaven. And the first voice which I heard was like a trumpet speaking with me, saying, 'Come up here, and I will show you things which must take place after this.' " This is the place of revelation.

But verse nine is the place I long for, a place where I can fall down and worship Him.

"Whenever the living creatures give glory and honor and thanks to Him who sits on the throne, who lives forever and ever, the twenty-four elders fall down before Him who sits on the throne and worship Him who lives forever and ever, and cast their crowns before the throne, saying: 'You are worthy, O Lord, To receive glory and honor and power; For You created all things, And by Your will they exist and were created.' " (Revelation 4:9)

You and I are invited to this place of INTIMACY, but we must leave the outer court.

You Are Special

This morning as I took the dogs out and was admiring our lilies, I couldn't help but have my breath taken away as I looked at the uniqueness and beauty of each flower. They are absolutely spectacular...

As I looked at them I thought of all of you. You are like these lilies. Each of you is unique and beautiful. As I pondered this, the thought came of just how special you are. I recalled Deuteronomy 7:6 (NLT): "For you are a holy people, who belong to the Lord your God. Of all the people on earth, the Lord your God has chosen you to be his own special treasure."

Did you see that? Abba has CHOSEN YOU... CHOSEN YOU TO BE HIS OWN SPECIAL TREASURE...

So many of us are seeking to feel valued. We want to feel special. I can hear a chorus of angels singing over you even now as I write this. Then suddenly I hear one distinct voice. As this one voice speaks, all the other voices become silent. I can see the angels kneeling as Abba speaks and His voice echoes through heaven and then throughout the entire earth. It is like a sound blast of a trumpet that permeates through every town, city, and village over the entire earth. There are no living creatures that can escape THE SOUND OF HIS VOICE. We who know Him or better stated, are known BY Him, hear, "I have chosen you."

If you listen carefully you can hear, "YOU ARE SPECIAL." I can see His eyes cascade over each of us. I don't know how He does it, but I see Him point at each of us at the same time declaring over each of us, YOU ARE MY VERY OWN SPECIAL TREASURE. Oh... YOU ARE SPECIAL...

Oh Lord, if only we could comprehend the majesty of these words. I can continue to hear Him not just declare, but actually sing over each of us - YOU ARE SPECIAL...

I'm Not Praying for Revival

That statement may have surprised you, but it's true. Instead of praying for revival I have decided to BE revival.

A number of years ago I was doing a night of ministry in an evangelical church. We were singing, and I didn't feel any anointing at all. The pastor turned to me and indicated that after the song finished it was time for me to minister. I looked up and told the Lord that I couldn't find Him there with a flashlight. In other words, I didn't sense the anointing. Immediately the Holy Spirit spoke to me and said, "If you don't carry the anointing, stay home."

That word has been such a blessing to me as I have traveled to so many places all over the world and not sensed the anointing. But the great news is that I don't have to sense it, I just have to carry it.

There is something I am praying for. I am praying for signs and wonders as the apostles did in Acts chapter four after Peter and John had been arrested. They got together to pray.

Acts 4:29-31: " 'Now Lord, look on their threats, and grant to Your servants that with all boldness they may speak Your word, by stretching out Your hand to heal, and that signs and wonders may be done through the name of Your holy Servant Jesus.' And when they had prayed, the place where they were assembled together was shaken; and they were all filled with the Holy Spirit, and they spoke the word of God with boldness."

The incredible news is that they didn't have to wait very long to see this prayer answered:

Acts 5:12-16: "And through the hands of the apostles many signs and wonders were done among the people. And they were all with one accord in Solomon's Porch. Yet none of the rest dared join them, but the people esteemed them highly. And believers were increasingly added to the Lord, multitudes of both men and women, so that they brought the sick out into the streets and laid them on beds and couches, that at least the shadow of Peter passing by might fall on some of them. Also a multitude gathered from the surrounding cities to Jerusalem, bringing sick people and those who were tormented by unclean spirits, and they were all healed."

I'm not praying for revival - I've decided to BE revival...

There is Nothing

That was the answer of Elijah's servant when he was sent to see if there were any signs of rain. If you remember, Elijah defeats the prophets of Baal on Mt Carmel. Instead of hanging around, Elijah goes higher on the mountain to pray in the promise that God had made to him earlier, that after three years of drought, rain would finally come.

There are times we need to pray in the promises of God. In Isaiah 43:26 (NKJV) God tells Isaiah, "Put Me in remembrance." What promises has God made you? Is it time to pray them in? Notice Elijah had to go higher on the mountain because he wanted to pray in the promise he had been given:

1 Kings 18:41-42: "Then Elijah said to Ahab, 'Go up, eat and drink; for there is the sound of abundance of rain.' So Ahab went up to eat and drink. And Elijah went up to the top of Carmel; then he bowed down on the ground, and put his face between his knees."

As Elijah prays, seven times he sends his servant to look toward the sea. Six times he comes back with the same answer - "There is nothing."

1 Kings 18:43: " 'Go up now, look toward the sea.' So he went up and looked, and said, 'There is nothing.' And seven times he said, 'Go again.' "

After hearing six times that nothing is happening, Elijah continues to pray. Why does he continue? Because he had a promise. Then something happened.

1 Kings 18:44-45: "Then it came to pass the seventh time, that he said, 'There is a cloud, as small as a man's hand, rising out of the sea!' So he said, 'Go up, say to Ahab,' "Prepare your chariot, and go down before the rain stops you." Now it happened in the meantime that the sky became black with clouds and wind, and there was a heavy rain."

Notice that he didn't wait for it to start raining before he declared it would rain. When we see something that seems insignificant, we shouldn't be discouraged – remember, something is about to happen.

Don't let the voice of "there's nothing happening" hinder you from pursuing your prophetic promise.

Habakkuk 2:3 (NKJV): "For the vision is yet for an appointed time; But at the end it will speak, and it will not lie. Though it tarries, wait for it; Because it will surely come, It will not tarry."

There is nothing - Don't believe it…

God is Assembling Young Leaders

Four years ago in Romania God gave me a word that I've since been carrying from church to church around the world.

The word comes from 1 Kings 20 where Ahab is surrounded by 32 kings of Syria and 140,00 troops.

A prophet suddenly appears to inform Ahab that God plans to defeat the Syrian armies. Ahab asks how and through whom? The answer? "Young leaders from different provinces."

1 Kings 20:13-15: "Suddenly a prophet approached Ahab king of Israel, saying, 'Thus says the Lord: "Have you seen all this great multitude? Behold, I will deliver it into your hand today, and you shall know that I am the Lord." So Ahab said, 'By whom?' And he said, 'Thus says the Lord: 'By the young leaders of the provinces.' "

"Then he said, 'Who will set the battle in order?' And he answered, 'You.' Then he mustered the young leaders of the provinces, and there were two hundred and thirty-two; and after them he mustered all the people, all the children of Israel—seven thousand."

If you are doing the math, this translates to 7232 verses 140,000, or 19.36 to 1.

It says the young leaders went out first, and then the army of 7000 followed.

1 Kings 20:17 (NKJV): "The young leaders of the provinces went out first." Verse 19: "Then these young leaders of the provinces went out of the city with the army which followed them."

This is what God is doing. He's assembling young men and women to be leaders in today's church…

God's About to Do Something

I know there's a cry in so many hearts like the cry from Habakkuk 1:2 (NKJV): "O Lord, how long shall I cry, And You will not hear?"

And I am fully persuaded that the answer God gave in verse five is the same thing He's saying today:

Habakkuk 1:5 (NKJV): "Look among the nations and watch—Be utterly astounded! For I will work a work in your days. Which you would not believe, though it were told you."

Message Bible - "Look around at the godless nations. Look long and hard. Brace yourself for a shock. Something's about to take place and you're going to find it hard to believe."

Did you notice that God said, "I will work a work in your days?" I am so excited about what God is doing and is about to do…

And do you know who God wants to use? Don't turn to look around, but instead, look in the mirror. IT'S YOU… How is that possible, you might ask. The answer is in:

Isaiah 60:1-3 (NKJV): "Arise, shine; For your light has come! And the glory of the Lord is risen upon you. For behold, the darkness shall cover the earth, And deep darkness the people; But the Lord will arise over you, And His glory will be seen upon you. The Gentiles shall come to your light, And kings to the brightness of your rising."

The Amplified Bible - "Arise [from spiritual depression to a new life], shine [be radiant with the glory and brilliance of the Lord]; for your light has come, And the glory and brilliance of the Lord has risen upon you. For in fact, darkness will cover the earth And deep darkness will cover the peoples; But the Lord will rise upon you [Jerusalem] And His glory and brilliance will be seen on you. "Nations will come to your light, And kings to the brightness of your rising."

It's time to arise and get rid of your spiritual depression. God's anointing is on you and He has and will continue to be in you and on you. And yes, people will see it and be drawn to it - drawn to you…

It's time to declare:

Isaiah 61:1-3 (NKJV): "The Spirit of the Lord God is upon Me, Because the Lord has anointed Me To preach good tidings to the poor; He has sent Me to heal the brokenhearted, To proclaim liberty to the captives, And the opening of the prison to those who are bound; To proclaim the acceptable year of the Lord, And the day of vengeance of our God; To comfort all who mourn, To console those who mourn in Zion, To give them beauty for ashes, The oil of joy for mourning."

God is about to do something, and yes, He'll do it through you…

Do We Have the Right Message?

That might seem like a weird question, but it's critical that we have the answer.

Turns out that we don't have to look too far – no further, in fact, then what Jesus Himself preached.

Luke 4:42 (NKJV): "Now when it was day, He departed and went into a deserted place. And the crowd sought Him and came to Him, and tried to keep Him from leaving them; but He said to them, 'I must preach the kingdom of God to the other cities also, because for this purpose I have been sent.' "

How clear is this? Jesus said that he had to preach the kingdom of God, because this was the purpose for which his Father sent him.

Matthew 4:23 (NKJV): "And Jesus went about all Galilee, teaching in their synagogues, preaching the gospel of the kingdom, and healing all kinds of sickness and all kinds of disease among the people."

The Greek word for preach means to proclaim/herald/announce. We are to herald/proclaim the Kingdom of God.

When Jesus sent out the twelve disciples, what did he say to them?

Luke 9:1-2 (NKJV): "Then He called His twelve disciples together and gave them power and authority over all demons, and to cure diseases. He sent them to preach the kingdom of God and to heal the sick."

When Jesus sent out the 70 disciples what did he say to them?

Luke 10:8-9 (NKJV): "Whatever city you enter, and they receive you, eat such things as are set before you. And heal the sick there, and say to them, 'The kingdom of God has come near to you.'"

Between the three gospels of Mark, Luke, and John, we see the Kingdom of God mentioned 68 times. In the Gospel of Matthew we find reference to the Kingdom of Heaven 32 times. That amounts to 100 mentions of the Kingdom of God with an additional 13 references in the rest of the New Testament.

The reason we are born again is to enter and see the Kingdom of God:

John 3:1-5 (NKJV): "There was a man of the Pharisees named Nicodemus, a ruler of the Jews. This man came to Jesus by night and said to Him, 'Rabbi, we know that You are a teacher come from God; for no one can do these signs that You do unless God is with him.' Jesus answered and said to him, 'Most assuredly, I say to you, unless one is born again, he cannot see the kingdom of God.' Nicodemus said to Him, 'How can a man be born when he is old? Can he enter a second time into his mother's womb and be born?' Jesus answered, 'Most assuredly, I say to you, unless one is born of water and the Spirit, he cannot enter the kingdom of God.' "

We are told to pray that God's kingdom will come, not later, but now.

Matthew 6:10 (NKJV): "Jesus taught us to pray, 'Thy kingdom come. Thy will be done in earth, as it is in heaven.' "

Then we have this powerful scripture telling us when the end will come.

Matthew 24:14 (NKJV): "And this gospel of the kingdom will be preached in all the world as a witness to all the nations, and then the end will come."

The Gospel of the Kingdom must be preached - that's our message.

We Haven't Been This Way Before

I believe we're in a similar place as Israel after Moses died and Joshua took over leadership. I believe God is raising up new leadership younger in both age and in spirit. Like Israel in Joshua chapter three, it's time to cross the Jordon River; it's time for the church to cross over into the promised land.

We read in Exodus 14:21 how Moses parted the Red Sea:

Exodus 14:21 (NKJV): "Moses stretched out his hand over the sea; and the Lord caused the sea to go back by a strong east wind all that night, and made the sea into dry land, and the waters were divided."

Joshua was probably thinking that Moses parted the Red Sea by stretching out his hand, so maybe he could do it the same way? Like him we often try to duplicate God's actions from the past, applying them to our current circumstances. We've probably discovered that doesn't usually work.

The word that Joshua sends through the camp is the word God spoke then and the same one He's speaking today:

Joshua 3:4 (NKJV) "...for you have not passed this way before."

Where the church is going is a route never before traveled. We'll need to discern what God wants to do and how He wants to do it – just like how the Jordon River was parted differently than was the Red Sea.

Joshua 3:12-17 (NKJV): " 'Now therefore, take for yourselves twelve men from the tribes of Israel, one man from every tribe. And it shall come to pass, as soon as the soles of the feet of the priests who bear the ark of the Lord, the Lord of all the earth, shall rest in the waters of the Jordan, that the waters of the Jordan shall be cut off, the waters that come down from upstream, and they shall stand as a heap.' So it was, when the people set out from their camp to cross over the Jordan, with the priests bearing the ark of the covenant before the people, and as those who bore the ark came to the Jordan, and the feet of the priests who bore the ark dipped in the edge of the water (for the Jordan overflows all its banks during the whole time of harvest), that the waters which came down from upstream stood still, and rose in a heap very far away at Adam, the city that is beside Zaretan. So the waters that went down into the Sea of the Arabah, the Salt Sea, failed, and were cut off; and the people crossed over opposite Jericho. Then the priests who bore the ark of the covenant of the Lord stood firm on dry ground in the midst of the Jordan; and all Israel crossed over on dry ground, until all the people had crossed completely over the Jordan."

It says the river stood still "as far away as the city of Adam." The City of Adam was 90 miles from where they were. Just imagine God stopping the water flow over a 90-mile distance!

Where we're going we haven't been before. We'll have new leadership and a new way of doing whatever the Lord wants us to do.

We haven't been this way before...

You Can't Send Someone Else to Do What You Are Called to Accomplish

In Second Kings chapter four we find the story of the Shunammite woman. If you remember the story, she had built a special room on her house for visiting prophets, and when Elisha stays with her he prophesies she'll have a son within the year. While at this point in the account she's unable to have children, one year later she gives birth to a son.

Some time passes, and the young lad falls ill, complaining about his head, and dies:

2 Kings 18:18-20: "And the child grew. Now it happened one day that he went out to his father, to the reapers. And he said to his father, 'My head, my head!' So he said to a servant, 'Carry him to his mother.' When he had taken him and brought him to his mother, he sat on her knees till noon, and then died."

In her grief the woman determines to find Elisha and so goes out to Mount Carmel to meet him. Once there she tells him everything that's happened, and Elisha decides to send Gehazi to raise the boy from the dead. Notice what happens:

2 Kings 4:29-31: "Then he said to Gehazi, 'Get yourself ready, and take my staff in your hand, and be on your way. If you meet anyone, do not greet him; and if anyone greets you, do not answer him; but lay my staff on the face of the child.' And the mother of the child said, 'As the Lord lives, and as your soul lives, I will not leave you.' So he arose and followed her. Now Gehazi went on ahead of them, and laid the staff on the face of the child; but there was neither voice nor hearing. Therefore he went back to meet him, and told him, saying, 'The child has not awakened.' "

Elisha sent Gehazi to do something he himself was called to do. Can you relate?

Listen, God is not interested in using somebody else. He has determined to use you. The rest of the story tells us that in the end Elisha does go, and the boy comes back to life.

God is calling you to bring life – You can't send someone else to do what God is calling you to accomplish.

A Decree Has Been Written

After the collapse of the Babylonian Empire, King Cyrus writes a decree saying that whatever Nebuchadnezzar has stolen from the temple has to be found and given back.

Ezra 6:1 (NKJV): "In the first year of King Cyrus, King Cyrus issued a decree concerning the house of God at Jerusalem."

Ezra 6:5 (NKJV): "Also let the gold and silver articles of the house of God, which Nebuchadnezzar took from the temple which is in Jerusalem and brought to Babylon, be restored and taken back to the temple which is in Jerusalem, each to its place; and deposit them in the house of God."

On New Year's Day this year, I asked the Lord what He wanted to do in the coming year, and He directed me to Ezra chapter six. As I read the pages I heard God say that He had issued a decree that whatever had been stolen from our church (that's you and me) had to be returned.

As we read Ezra chapter six we see that the items that were stolen were in fact, returned, and that the Temple in Jerusalem was restored and rededicated.

That's exactly what I see happening today. God's temple is being restored, and we'll dedicate ourselves to God's purposes.

I was impressed that the giving back of what the enemy has stolen will begin in 2018 and will continue through the following years until everything is returned.

A decree has been written...

Our Excuses are Being Canceled

A number of years ago I was struggling with something and kept on making excuses about why I couldn't do what God was asking me to do.

We're so much like our parents Adam and Eve. When God confronts them over their sin they don't hesitate to offer excuses. Adam scapegoats his wife, and Eve blames the devil. Does that sound like something we've done or perhaps are still doing - blaming others or the devil?

I don't remember exactly where I was, but to this day I can still see the vision God gave me. I was riding a train to Boston as I might have experienced it some years ago. It was customary then for the conductor to walk through the aisles punching holes in the passengers' tickets. So it was here.

God said, "That's what I'm doing with all your excuses." I then saw the same conductor ask me for my ticket again, and as he stood beside my seat, he began to use his hole punch to eliminate every excuse. Then after what I perceived were several minutes (lots of excuses), he handed the ticket back to me and told me to keep it. As I looked at the ticket, every excuse represented had a hole through it.

I wonder what we could accomplish as the body of Christ if we didn't have any excuses?

About the same time God gave me this vision, I happened to come across

John 14:30 (NKJV), which says:

"I will no longer talk much with you, for the ruler of this world is coming, and he has nothing in Me."

Jesus is saying that Satan was coming to try and accuse him of something he had done wrong. Jesus said that there wasn't anything in his life that Satan could find to accuse him of or any sin in his life.

I don't know about you, but I wouldn't be able to claim the same thing. I am striving towards that, though. I want to one day be able to say, "for the ruler of this world is coming, and he has nothing in Me."

Thank God – our excuses are being cancelled.

Going-the-Second-Mile Principle

In Matthew 5:41 (NKJV) we read, "And whoever compels you to go one mile, go with him two."

What does this mean?

The following is from an article in a commentary from Making Life Count Ministries. It does a great job explaining what Jesus meant.

"Cyrus the Great, the king of Persia, invented the postal system to carry letters and documents from one place to another. To make his system work, any courier could force anyone to carry the mail for one mile, but only one mile. The Romans adopted this system for their military to keep their soldiers from getting worn out from carrying heavy backpacks, which weighed about 66 pounds. Roman soldiers could compel any Jew to carry his backpack for one mile. Roman roads had mile markers similar to the mile markers we have today on Interstate highways, so it was easy to know where each mile started and ended. If someone refused to do it, he would be flogged."

If you think about it, Jesus was asking them to go at least four miles - two miles in one direction and two miles back.

So what does all this mean? Today more than ever, it seems increasingly difficult to get people in church to volunteer. Normally there are the people who are always doing something, and then a larger number who for whatever reason, are not serving at all. I read twice in the Bible:

Mark 10:45 and Matthew 20:28 (NKJV): "For even the Son of Man did not come to be served, but to serve, and to give His life a ransom for many."

That's it - we were created to serve. Jesus is our ultimate example. We are asked to go the extra mile, and we need to do it willingly and gladly, as doing it with the wrong spirit has no life in it. We've all experienced people doing something for us begrudgingly, with the wrong attitude and spirit, and we end up wishing they'd never done it at all.

The church needs everyone to serve gladly, something we read about in the letter to the Ephesians:

Ephesians 4:16 (NKJV): "...from whom the whole body, joined and knit together by what every joint supplies, according to the effective working by which every part does its share, causes growth of the body for the edifying of itself in love."

Yes, every one of us needs to serve somewhere, and in the manner of the second-mile principle, to go willingly, and do above and beyond what we're asked to do.

This principle works in every situation. Imagine your boss asking you to clean one room, and you go on to clean several. You're asked to come early, and you volunteer to stay late.

Let's go beyond. Let's walk the second mile.

You Are a Masterpiece

Ever since I became a son of God, the Lord put a love for people in my heart.

I loved people, but to be truthful, didn't always honor or value them. More often than not I would see flaws, weaknesses, and peculiarities before I saw anything else.

There were lots of reasons for this, and you might presume that this attitude would have been healed and adjusted within a few years of my conversion. Think again. In need of healing from my past, my tendency to view things through the lens of the law needed to be shed. Until then I failed to value and honor.

First Peter 2:17 instructs us to "honor all people." I had read this but failed to apply it. Ephesians 2:10 was the key. I read the New Living Translation version of this scripture and then researched it in the Greek, and my whole life and perspective changed.

From the New King James version:

Ephesians 2:10: "For we are His workmanship, created in Christ Jesus for good works, which God prepared beforehand that we should walk in them."

Then from the New Living Translation:

Ephesians 2:10: "For we are God's masterpiece. He has created us anew in Christ Jesus, so we can do the good things he planned for us long ago."

If we were to go to an art museum we would see famous paintings by Rembrandt, Vincent van Gogh, Pablo Ruiz Picasso, Leonardo da Vinci, Michelangelo, and others. Gazing at them we would stand in awe, overwhelmed by their character and beauty. Our mouths might even open in an attempt to express both honor and wonder.

By the grace and kindness of God, my perspective has changed. I now see others as "masterpieces" created to fulfill God's plans for their lives and to impact His Kingdom.

I want to tell you – you are a MASTERPIECE.

Desire Spiritual Gifts, But Especially That You May Prophesy

Since 1981 I have seen lives supernaturally changed – seemingly before my eyes - through a simple prophetic word.

Even after 39 years I continue to be in awe of how the Holy Spirit can heal, deliver, breathe hope, break off depression, discouragement and every evil thing with just a few words. I have seen entire families changed, marriages restored, dreams and visions confirmed, gifts and anointing imparted, and much, much more.

Perhaps my life scripture is 1 Samuel 10:6 (NKJV): "Then the Spirit of the Lord will come upon you, and you will prophesy with them and be turned into another man." This was the word Samuel gave to Saul when he was to come among the prophets. It is promised that the Holy Spirit will come on a person. The scripture doesn't say if, it says when. When God's Spirit comes on you, you will prophesy (breathe life), and you will be changed into another man.

Prophetic ministry changes lives. It will also cause people to draw closer to God and to fall down and worship.

1 Corinthians 14:25 (NKJV) says that when someone prophesies that

"the secrets of his heart are revealed; and so, falling down on his face, he will worship God and report that God is truly among you."

1 Corinthians 14:1 (NKJV): "Pursue love, and desire spiritual gifts, but especially that you may prophesy."

In 1981 while visiting an older woman who was sick I spoke my first prophetic word. Then again and again and again. I started out giving very generic words, but then they became more specific. Like any gift it had to be exercised in order for it to grow.

Romans 12:6 (NKJV): "Having then gifts differing according to the grace that is given to us, let us use them: if prophecy, let us prophesy in proportion to our faith."

Here is a brief word about spiritual gifts: Notice the diversity of gifts, that they operate differently in each person:

1 Corinthians 12:1-11 (NKJV): "Now concerning spiritual gifts, brethren, I do not want you to be ignorant: You know that you were Gentiles, carried away to these dumb[b] idols, however you were led. Therefore I make known to you that no one speaking by the Spirit of God calls Jesus [c]accursed, and no one can say that Jesus is Lord except by the Holy Spirit. There are diversities of gifts, but the same Spirit. There are differences of ministries, but the same Lord. And there are diversities of activities, but it is the same God who works all in all. But the manifestation of the Spirit is given to each one for the profit of all: for to one is given the word of wisdom through the Spirit, to another the word of knowledge through the same Spirit, to another faith by the same Spirit, to another gifts of healings by the same Spirit, to another the working of miracles, to another prophecy, to another discerning of spirits, to another different kinds of tongues, to another the interpretation of tongues. But one and the same Spirit works all these things, distributing to each one individually as He wills."

Each gift given by the Holy Spirit is, as it says in verse seven, for everyone's benefit. Each of God's gifts is amazing in its own right, in its impact on people's lives, and we are told as the scripture says, to "desire spiritual gifts," but especially that we "may prophesy."

God will use you to change lives forever...

Don't Let the Fire Go Out

First, we must agree that each of us who has given our life to the Lord is a son or daughter of God. Secondly, agree that we are the priests of today - not just ordained people, but priests.

We must comprehend this so we may take our place in God's plan for this appointed time. Each of us is to play a key role in what the Holy Spirit is doing today, equipping us to reign on the earth with Christ as God's Kingdom comes. Read below:

Revelation 1:6 (NKJV): "...and has made us kings and priests to His God and Father, to Him be glory and dominion forever and ever. Amen."

Revelation 5:10 (NKJV): "And have made us kings and priests to our God; And we shall reign on the earth."

Revelation 21:1-4 (NKJV): "Now I saw a new heaven and a new earth, for the first heaven and the first earth had passed away. Also, there was no more sea. Then I, John, saw the holy city, New Jerusalem, coming down out of heaven from God, prepared as a bride adorned for her husband. And I heard a loud voice from heaven saying, 'Behold, the tabernacle of God is with men, and He will dwell with them, and they shall be His people. God Himself will be with them and be their God. And God will wipe away every tear from their eyes; there shall be no more death, nor sorrow, nor crying. There shall be no more pain, for the former things have passed away.' "

Part of our responsibility is to ensure that God's fire doesn't go out.

Leviticus 6:12 (NKJV): "And the fire on the altar shall be kept burning on it; it shall not be put out. And the priest shall burn wood on it every morning."

If we were living at the time when the book of Leviticus was written, what would we think of priests who allowed the fire to go out?

Even as I'm writing this I instinctively bow my head in humility and pray.

"Oh Lord, I am here to bring my prayers to you as my morning offering. I am bringing worship and adoration that your fire may not go out. Father, let your fire spread through every town, village, and city throughout the world."

One of the ways to keep the fire burning is to remember that we're appointed to carry God's fire wherever we go.

Here the cry of the Spirit – Don't let the fire of God go out!

Not Called to Sweat

This sounds weird! Is this phrase even in the Bible, you might ask? And if it is, what can it possibly mean?

Here's the verse where God speaks to the sons of Zadok. He recognized them as faithful priests during Israel's rebellion at a time when many of the other priests were turning to idol worship. Here is His instruction to them to not sweat.

Ezekiel 44:15-19 (NKJV): " 'But the priests, the Levites, the sons of Zadok, who kept charge of My sanctuary when the children of Israel went astray from Me, they shall come near Me to minister to Me; and they shall stand before Me to offer to Me the fat and the blood,' says the Lord God. 'They shall enter My sanctuary, and they shall come near My table to minister to Me, and they shall keep My charge. And it shall be, whenever they enter the gates of the inner court, that they shall put on linen garments; no wool shall come upon them while they minister within the gates of the inner court or within the house. They shall have linen turbans on their heads and linen trousers on their bodies; they shall not clothe themselves with anything that causes sweat. When they go out to the outer court, to the outer court to the people, they shall take off their garments in which they have ministered, leave them in the holy chambers, and put on other garments; and in their holy garments they shall not sanctify the people.' "

I don't recall the year when I first read that verse, but it was life changing. At the time I was running around feeling obligated to fulfill my call and be sure that I was serving God with my whole self. This meant working in the church close to 75 hours a week, and in the process, yes, sweating, and fairly profusely. Run here, run there, do this, do that, see this person, and then that person.

After a time, however, the Holy Spirit said, "Stop sweating; it's time to do things differently."

I did! Over a period of a few months I adjusted my schedule as much as I was able, but discovered that it was more than just a difference in time management; it was actually a transformation of my heart. I realized that being busy was my way of getting approval. Like so many others, I had performance mentality. Performing and achievement were ways I assigned value to myself, so the busier I was, the more valuable I perceived myself.

At the same time I was processing this I read Luke chapter four where Satan wants Jesus to perform. On top of that I realized that I was created to rest. In fact, man's first day on earth was the seventh day, the day of rest.

Luke 4:3 (NKJV): "And the devil said to Him, 'If You are the Son of God, command this stone to become bread.' "

Exodus 33:14 (NKJV): "And He said, 'My Presence will go with you, and I will give you rest.' "

We were created and called to be sons and daughters who are living and carrying His presence while resting, not sweating. From the sons of Zadok we get the picture of changing our garments – is there a message here for us?

It's simple - DON'T SWEAT…

I Wish to See Jesus

This was the cry of some Gentiles who'd come to the feast. Is that not our cry too?

Though these particular Gentiles had converted to Judaism, something else was burning in their hearts. They knew there was more, that Jesus was at the very center of what they were seeking.

John 12:20-22 (NKJV): "Now there were certain Greeks among those who came up to worship at the feast. Then they came to Philip, who was from Bethsaida of Galilee, and asked him, saying, 'Sir, we wish to see Jesus.' Philip came and told Andrew, and in turn, Andrew and Philip told Jesus."

It took some time to find Jesus, and his response is fascinating.

John 14:23-28 (NKJV): "But Jesus answered them, saying, 'The hour has come that the Son of Man should be glorified. Most assuredly, I say to you, unless a grain of wheat falls into the ground and dies, it remains alone; but if it dies, it produces much grain. He who loves his life will lose it, and he who hates his life in this world will keep it for eternal life. If anyone serves Me, let him follow Me; and where I am, there My servant will be also. If anyone serves Me, him My Father will honor.' "

Jesus tells them that if they want to see him, there will be a price. The same holds true for us.

The natural/carnal man cannot receive the things of the Spirit. If we really want to get a revelation of Jesus, then our flesh and will must die. While over the years I've recognized the desire and hunger of countless great people, in the end they just weren't willing to give their whole selves.

I wish to see Jesus, you say. That's wonderful; you'll have to abandon your flesh... I can tell you it's worth the price, though it may be painful...

God's Not in a Hurry

Just ask all the people who heard Isaiah prophesy that the Messiah was coming. Isaiah prophesied for approximately 64 years during the reign of four different kings - Uzziah, Jotham, Ahaz, and Hezekiah, and therefore became known as the Messianic Prophet, He prophesied 700 years in advance of Christ's birth.

According to many historians there are 365 prophecies in the Old Testament pertaining to Christ as the coming Messiah – one for every day of the year. The oldest among them is found in Genesis 3:15:

Genesis 3:15 (NKJV): "And I will put enmity Between you and the woman, And between your seed and her Seed; He shall bruise your head, And you shall bruise His heel."

You can yell, scream, complain, and pray, yet more often than not you won't change God's mind. Listen, I have done all of the above, even fasting 21 days at a time only to get an answer other than the one I was expecting. It was only after years and years that I came to understand the phrase "appointed time."

It was in 1987 when I started reminding God that I had been given a word in 1970 that I would one day have my own church. He told me he wasn't finished working on me. As much as I prayed and fasted, I couldn't change God's mind because He has His appointed time. Five years later in 1992 I was released to start my own church.

Thirty-three times we find the phrase "appointed time."

Genesis 18:14 (NKJV): "Is anything too hard for the Lord? At the appointed time I will return to you, according to the time of life, and Sarah shall have a son."

Habakkuk 2:3 (NKJV): "For the vision is yet for an appointed time;

But at the end it will speak, and it will not lie. Though it tarries, wait for it; Because it will surely come, It will not tarry."

Since God is outside of time and therefore never in a hurry, it's vital to capture the moment and what He's doing in the present. Too often we focus on the opposite. So be at peace; there is an APPOINTED TIME…

Which Kingdom?

When you wake up in the morning there are two kingdoms in your bedroom. There is the Kingdom of God ruled by the Prince of Peace (Isaiah 9:6), and The Kingdom of This World ruled by the prince of the power of the air (Ephesians 2:2).

There is a choice to be made as to which kingdom you're going to engage and which prince you'll end up yielding to.

Most people get up in the morning and just start doing life. You know – the routine of using the bathroom, making coffee, getting dressed, waking the kids, and then leaving for work, before which may come a short prayer telling God what He has to do. Such is entering The Kingdom of World by Default.

Believe it or not there's another choice. When you open your eyes and before you jump out of bed, say, "Good Morning, Father. I am looking forward to walking with you today. Would you lead me and teach me?"

Rather than just launching into your typical routine, perhaps you could plan to wake up 30 minutes early so you can have time with God. Take a few minutes to worship (with the help of YouTube perhaps) and a few minutes just to chat. In this manner, which Kingdom have you now engaged?

The words God spoke to Moses ring in my ears:

Deuteronomy 30:19 (NKJV): "I call heaven and earth as witnesses today against you, that I have set before you life and death, blessing and curses; therefore choose life, that both you and your descendants may live."

So which Kingdom will you choose?

Created to Live in His Presence

We can all picture Adam walking with God in the Garden of Eden, Eden meaning in Hebrew "presence," a term which to even say or write creates overwhelming excitement in me.

I used to be jealous reading the following scriptures, until one day God told me that Jesus had restored all the rights lost by Adam and Eve and that I too, could literally walk with God every day, just as you can.

Genesis 5:22 (NKJV): "Enoch walked with God three hundred years."

Genesis 6:9 (NKJV): "This is the genealogy of Noah. Noah was a just man, perfect in his generations. Noah walked with God."

Listen – you were created to walk with God…

It's Time to Shoot Our Cows

In the Old Testament there are numerous references to Israel worshipping the image of calves. While today we might not worship calves per se, we may instead be guilty of worshipping other things that are more valuable to us than obedience to God's word.

Psalm 106:19 (NKJV): "They made a calf in Horeb, And worshiped the molded image.

Exodus 32:7-8 (NKJV): "And the Lord said to Moses, 'Go, get down! For your people whom you brought out of the land of Egypt have corrupted themselves. They have turned aside quickly out of the way which I commanded them. They have made themselves a molded calf, and worshiped it and sacrificed to it, and said, "This is your god, O Israel, that brought you out of the land of Egypt!" ' "

So what do I mean by the phrase, "It's time to shoot our cows?"

Cows represent opinions or other things in our lives that we value more than our obedience to the Lord. Are there things that the Holy Spirit has been pointing to and asking us to change in our lives, but we've been resistant?

Well, say hello to your sacred cow. The Holy Spirit talks to you about your giving, yet you refuse to respond. Say hello to your sacred cow. You have unforgiveness in your heart which you don't want to release. Say hello to your sacred cow.

Recently while I was in Romania I had a vision come to me when I was preaching. I saw angels going into a building similar to a garage or shed. Hanging on the walls were rifles. The angels grabbed the rifles, went out into the field, and began shooting sacred cows. When I relayed the details of the vision, the room erupted in laughter, but it really wasn't meant to be humorous. God wants to eliminate anything in our lives that we value more than obedience to Him and to His word…

Perhaps you can take a moment and ask the Lord what cows might be mooing in your personal backyard?

What's Your Vision?

I've seen countless people who lost their vision, had it stolen, or simply abandoned it. The result is a short period of aimless living.

The passion and zeal they once had is gone, like a fire that's been put out. Sadly, compromise soon begins creeping in. The anointing which was so evident on their lives begins to wane until there is little or none left.

Proverbs 29:18 (ASV): "Where there is no vision, the people cast off restraint."

(CSB) "Without revelation people run wild."

(TPT) "When there is no clear prophetic vision, people quickly wander astray."

If you have lost your vision, then rekindle it. You say, but that vision is impossible to rekindle. Okay, so get a new one... It's never too late. Moses was 80 when after 40 years he stepped into his vision. Caleb was 85 when after 45 years he said, "Give me this mountain." (Joshua 14:12)

Whatever lies the devil has told you, it's time you tell him to shut up. God's bigger than our past. Our Father has need of you... He hasn't changed his mind about you. You're unique. You're one of a kind. There are people only you can touch, only you can reach...

Write your vision, pray about it, spend time talking to the Lord about it. Water it like a seed. Lastly, make sure it gets a lot of "son."

It's never too late...you are needed.

Can You Pick on Someone Else?

Yes, I have said that to God on a number of occasions.

There have been times in my life with trial after trial, and I thought that God was working on me and giving everyone else a pass. At those times I told Him that I couldn't take any more and then… things got worse. I'd quote 1 Corinthians 10:13, saying, "Okay; but you told me that you wouldn't allow 'the temptation to be more than I could stand' well, we are there now, and I can't take any more."

And again… things got worse… Funny, but here is the entirety of 1 Corinthians 10:13. It says,

"The temptations in your life are no different from what others experience. And God is faithful. He will not allow the temptation to be more than you can stand. When you are tempted, he will show you a way out so that you can endure." (NLT)

Then I would be reminded of 1 Peter 4:12 (NKJV):

"Beloved, do not think it strange concerning the fiery trial which is to try you, as though some strange thing happened to you."

Then if that wasn't enough, there is:

Psalm 34:19 (NKJV): "Many are the afflictions of the righteous, But the Lord delivers him out of them all."

On top of all those I would hear, "You wanted to be more like me. You want to carry 'power.' In order to carry my power, you need character. Everything you are going through is an answer to your prayer and yes, the call of God on your life."

After that came Philippians 2:13 which says,

"For God is working in you, giving you the desire and the power to do what pleases him." (NLT)

So the next time you feel like God is picking on you, know that…He IS! He is fashioning you more into His likeness so you won't be a reflection of yourself, but of Him.

There is an old song we used to sing called "Refiner's Fire." Here are the lyrics:

Purify my heart

Let me be as gold and precious silver

Purify my heart

Let me be as gold, pure gold

Refiner's fire

My heart's one desire

Is to be holy

Set apart for You, Lord

I choose to be holy

Set apart for You, my Master

Ready to do Your will

Purify my heart

Cleanse me from within

And make me holy

Purify my heart

Cleanse me from my sin

Deep within:

Father, thank you that you are working in us even when we don't want you to.

Our desire to represent Christ's character and power is all it comes down to.

Praise God that He is working in us!

What Did Jesus Mean, Turn the Other Cheek?

"But I tell you not to resist an evil person. But whoever slaps you on your right cheek, turn the other to him also." (Matthew 5:39, NKJV)

Was Jesus saying abuse is okay? Certainly not… I want to make that abundantly clear. We are never to hit or slap our wives or husbands or children or for that matter, any other person at all. And I'm not talking about the cases where we need to defend ourselves. I'm instead referring to those times when we may be tempted to hit someone else in anger.

Here is what James 1:20 (NKJV) says,

"for the wrath of man does not produce the righteousness of God."

Then Romans 12:18 (NKJV):

"If it is possible, as much as depends on you, live peaceably with all men."

Turning the cheek is not a literal truth but points instead to an attitude of the heart. Jesus is saying that when someone hurts us we must have a willingness to not abandon the relationship. I'm not talking about burying our head in the sand and ignoring real issues but making every effort - if the other person is willing - to work it through with them.

Remember, Paul writes:

2 Corinthians 5:18 (NKJV): "God has given us the ministry of reconciliation."

What happens is that we tend to focus on the people who've hurt us instead of thinking about the people who we have hurt.

Turning the cheek means to be willing to work out and work through the hurt or offense in a biblical manner, thus healing and restoring the relationship.

Oh, a couple of other verses to help us process:

Psalm 130:3 (CSB): "Lord, if you kept an account of iniquities, Lord, who could stand?"

Matthew 18:21-22 (NKJV): "Then Peter came to Him and said, 'Lord, how often shall my brother sin against me, and I forgive him? Up to seven times?' Jesus said to him, 'I do not say to you, up to seven times, but up to seventy times seven.' "

I didn't say this was easy, but in reality "doing the truth" is our only option...

There Were Two Prodigal Sons

We are all familiar with the story of the prodigal son written about in Luke chapter 15. But did you know that there wasn't just one prodigal, but two? The second was the older brother.

By definition, a prodigal exhibits wasteful living, the root of his behavior originating in the heart. When our heart isn't right it produces various forms of conduct. In this case one son went out and lived a sinful life style, while the oldest son stayed home, his sinful heart unexposed until his brother's return. In reading the account of the older brother, something becomes very clear about the condition of his heart.

Before I quote the verses it's important to know that the oldest son failed to fulfill his obligations. It was customary that the oldest son was the one with the primary responsibility to carry out his father's wishes. If a party was given it was the role of the oldest brother to be the host and to ensure that all his father's plans were carried out to the letter.

Is it becoming clear to you that the second prodigal lived at home with rebellion in his heart while the youngest son expressed his rebellion in the open?

Luke 15:11-32: "Now his older son was in the field. And as he came and drew near to the house, he heard music and dancing. So he called one of the servants and asked what these things meant. And he said to him, 'Your brother has come, and because he has received him safe and sound, your father has killed the fatted calf.'

But he was angry and would not go in. Therefore his father came out and pleaded with him. So he answered and said to his father, 'Lo, these many years I have been serving you; I never transgressed your commandment at any time; and yet you never gave me a young goat, that I might make merry with my friends. But as soon as this son of yours came, who has devoured your livelihood with harlots, you killed the fatted calf for him.' And he said to him, 'Son, you are always with me, and all that I have is yours. It was right that we should make merry and be glad, for your brother was dead and is alive again, and was lost and is found.' "

We see in this exchange that the older brother has a terrible attitude. He is self-righteous, resentful, and jealous, and also has an issue with his father, hiding his rebellion and refusing to obey him. He is blind to his own sin, claiming, "I never transgressed your commandment at any time."

Yes, there were two prodigals, and the father (also our Father), loved them both unconditionally.

The story of the older brother might be more relatable to some yet harder to grasp. While the older brother doesn't go out and live a riotous life, he has his own heart issues, issues hidden from the surface but just as dangerous. The result is that he misses completely the unconditional love of the Father.

So tell me: is there some of the older brother in you?

Shopping Cart Christianity

Picture yourself in a grocery store. You walk in and grab a shopping cart and then proceed to go up and down the aisles selecting things you want. Some items are healthier and better for you, but you just push your cart past those items, while others you know you shouldn't put in, you do anyway.

You have to admit that this is a prophetic picture of what a lot of Christianity looks like. I just got a picture of the Lord watching the cameras in the store. He sits there and like a good Father is saying out loud, "DON'T PUT THAT IN YOUR CART, AND OH, PLEASE PUT THAT BACK AND MAKE A BETTER CHOICE…"

Here are two good words of counsel:

Proverbs 3:6 (NKJV): "In all your ways acknowledge Him, And He shall [a]direct your paths.

Deuteronomy 30:19 (NKJV): "I call heaven and earth as witnesses today against you, that I have set before you life and death, blessing and cursing; therefore choose life, that both you and your descendants may live."

I know that compromise creates so many problems. We know what is right at times, but like the ostrich, conveniently stick our heads in the sand. Or maybe we can relate to Sargent Schultz from the television series Hogan's Heroes, when to avoid confrontation he'd say, "I see nothing."

One final word of wisdom.

Deuteronomy 6:18 (NKJV): "And you shall do what is right and good in the sight of the Lord, that it may be well with you, and that you may go in and possess the good land of which the Lord swore to your fathers."

Lord, help us to live out this verse in our daily lives!

Having the Spirit of a Centurion

Did you know there is a direct correlation between true faith and understanding authority?

We seem to be in the season of the church when people are struggling with authority. It looks like this current climate has raised a generation who find yielding to authority difficult. This may be because over the past 25 or so years an imbalance occurred in this area. During this period a pastor would say, "Jump!" and the desired response was "How high?" It was considered rebellion if a person questioned an instruction or said they didn't understand.

The church, like any organization, is often like a pendulum. It swings from one extreme to another, far to the left and then far to the right. Applied to the view of the pastorate, the swing in many churches took the form of people having little respect for those in this position. Because he was hired, he was seen to have the position not because God appointed him, but because he was voted in. The effect was that if the pastor wanted to accomplish a certain goal or had a certain vision, the church board and congregation often refused to respond to what he said. He was their "buddy," not their pastor.

So right after the Jesus Movement it became clear that a better understanding of pastoral authority was needed. And so the teaching began. Unfortunately much of it was rooted in the Old Testament, thus altogether missing the heart of God. This mindset of authority then spread through the whole church - to elders, deacons, and heads of ministries.

We needed to look instead at the example of Jesus (the ultimate authority) to see how he taught and mentored his disciples. First Peter 2:21 (NKJV) gives us the heart we need. It says that Jesus left us an example that we "should follow His steps." Our ultimate goal is to be a leader like him. Paul was such a leader, pouring his life out for his fellow believers and giving all pastors and leaders today an example of the right heart.

Being a centurion doesn't mean having no voice or following blindly. It means expressing ourselves respectfully and in the right way, seeking balance, not blindness.

Like with so many things in the body of Christ, we're continuing to learn and to "grow in grace and knowledge." Wherever I go I always tell the pastor that I am a centurion, there under their authority. The following verses about faith and authority have a lot to teach us, but if there's no willingness to change and see how they apply to us personally then we'll miss the cry of God's heart.

Here's Matthew 8:5-10:

"Now when Jesus had entered Capernaum, a centurion came to Him, pleading with Him, saying, 'Lord, my servant is lying at home paralyzed, dreadfully tormented.' And Jesus said to him, 'I will come and heal him.' The centurion answered and said, 'Lord, I am not worthy that You should come under my roof. But only speak a word, and my servant will be healed. For I also am a man under authority, having soldiers under me. And I say to this one, 'Go,' and he goes; and to another, 'Come,' and he comes; and to my servant, 'Do this,' and he does it. When Jesus heard it, He marveled, and said to those who followed, 'Assuredly, I say to you, I have not found such great faith, not even in Israel!' " (NKJV)

The centurion knew beyond a doubt that when Jesus said something, that something would happen. Here in this story Jesus didn't pray for healing, he just spoke it. This was not a new concept.

Psalm 107:20 (NKJV): "He sent His word and healed them."

When we understand the authority of Jesus' name we'll begin to see miracles on a regular basis. Since we lack the heart to joyfully submit to authority, however, we are robbed of its benefit. If we wish to operate with a greater anointing of authority we must be willing to be under it. And if we want authority, we must be under authority. Even if that person is like Saul - David still yielded.

James was right when he wrote:

"But do you want to know, O foolish man, that faith without works is dead?" (James 2:20, NKJV)

You want greater authority, then yield to authority...

Being Fully Persuaded

In today's church there are a variety of doctrines. Some churches allow certain things, while others are opposed to what other churches are doing. One church follows something as truth, and another church calls that same thing error. Who's right?

The challenge for each of us is to decide for ourselves. This admonition is presented in Romans 14:5 (NKJV) where it says, "One person esteems one day above another; another esteems every day alike. Let each be fully convinced in his own mind." Paul is talking here about how some believers were keeping the Old Testament Holy Days and others were not. He told them that they needed to make up their own minds and be fully persuaded about their decisions.

This principle holds true in every area of our life. Elijah puts it this way:

"And Elijah came to all the people, and said, 'How long will you falter between two opinions?' " (1Kings 18:2 NKJV)

When we can't make up our mind, we end up fulfilling what James says about a "double-minded man," who is "unstable in all his ways." (James 1:8, NKJV)

The church is in desperate need of people who believe what they believe, not because someone else believes it, but because they've proven it for themselves. If this is the case, then when the storms of life come, and they do come, we're able to stand firm because we know what we know because it's our truth, not someone else's.

In the days ahead, Satan is going to pull out all the stops. It will be crucial that each of us can apply:

1 Thessalonians 5 :21 (NKJV): "Test all things; hold fast what is good."

Make your mind up to be fully persuaded in what you believe and why you believe it...

Walk in What You Know, Not in What You Don't Know

We're all learning to walk in the Spirit and are at different places on this journey.

One of my greatest mistakes for many years was trying to be somewhere I wasn't. It often stole my peace and created conflict in my head and in my Spirit. For example, as I was just talking about this principle with someone, I heard a baby cry. The prophetic picture was about expecting something way before its time. A newborn can't even hold its head up, never mind crawl.

All too often we want to be in a place but we just aren't old enough, wise enough, or mature enough to be there. You don't hand a baseball to a twelve-year old and ask them to throw it 100 miles an hour. Yes, the twelve-year old may acknowledge that a professional baseball pitcher can throw a baseball at that speed, but even with that, the fact is that only a tiny handful of them can throw a baseball that fast.

The point is that we can only do what we're equipped and empowered to do at any given point in time. We have to walk in the anointing/gift/ability we have in the moment, trying not be somewhere else.

Why do you think Jesus sent them out and then took them aside privately? It was to teach, train and mentor them.

Luke 9:1: "Then He called His twelve disciples together and gave them power and authority over all demons, and to cure diseases. He sent them to preach the kingdom of God and to heal the sick."

Then verse 10:

"And the apostles, when they had returned, told Him all that they had done. Then He took them and went aside privately into a deserted place belonging to the city called Bethsaida."

Luke 10:1: "After these things the Lord appointed [a]seventy others also, and sent them two by two before His face into every city and place where He Himself was about to go."

Then they return:

"Then the seventy returned with joy, saying, 'Lord, even the demons are subject to us in Your name.' And He said to them, 'I saw

Satan fall like lightning from heaven. Behold, I give you the authority to trample on serpents and scorpions, and over all the power of the enemy, and nothing shall by any means hurt you. Nevertheless do not rejoice in this, that the spirits are subject to you, but rather rejoice because your names are written in heaven.' " (verse 17)

There's the simple reality that we are here today functioning in today's anointing, ability, and gifting. We cannot walk in tomorrow's, never mind next week's or next year's.

Enjoy where you are… Tomorrow will come soon enough.

Dead Men Don't Have Earthly Rights

We are faced with a decision. Do we want to cling to and hold onto our earthly rights or do we want to cling to our heavenly ones? By holding onto our earthly rights, we're relinquishing the rights to our heavenly ones.

I can hold onto my anger and unforgiveness, feelings associated with my earthly rights. I may insist, "I was hurt and betrayed so I have a right to be full of anger and bitterness and to want revenge because that person lied about me." We can say and even believe these things, but by clinging to these rights we shouldn't be surprised that we're going to be unhappy and our whole life upside down.

Or… we can realize that when we were baptized, we were baptized into the death of Christ, and when we came out from the water we came out as a brand-new creature. Our heavenly rights are now righteousness, peace, and joy.

When we step back and look at it logically, do we want to be happy or miserable?

Paul tells us we are dead but simultaneously alive:

Romans 6:4 (NKJV): "Therefore we were buried with Him through baptism into death, that just as Christ was raised from the dead by the glory of the Father, even so we also should walk in newness of life."

Romans 6:11(NKJV): "Likewise you also, reckon yourselves to be dead indeed to sin, but alive to God in Christ Jesus our Lord."

So which do you want - your earthly or your heavenly rights?

God Hid it From Me

It is true. Jesus said in John 10:10 "that my sheep hear my voice."

I believe if we pray God will answer:

Jeremiah 33:3 (NKJV): "Call to Me, and I will answer you, and show you great and mighty things, which you do not know."

I believe that God delights to show us things:

Revelation 4:1 (NKJV): "After these things I looked, and behold, a door standing open in heaven. And the first voice which I heard was like a trumpet speaking with me, saying, 'Come up here, and I will show you things which must take place after this.' "

But scripture also teaches that at times He holds back:

It could be John 16:12 (NKJV): "I still have many things to say to you, but you cannot bear them now."

Even when the Shunammite woman's son dies, and she goes to tell Elisha, Elisha doesn't know why she's come, even though he's a prophet:

2 Kings 4:27: "Now when she came to the man of God at the hill, she caught him by the feet, but Gehazi came near to push her away. But the man of God said, 'Let her alone; for her soul is in deep distress, and the Lord has hidden it from me, and has not told me.' "

Even though at times I'm frustrated when He hides things from me, I'm nevertheless thankful for this verse. It reminds me of the movie "A Few Good Men." There's a scene when Jack Nicholson is on the witness stand and Tom Cruise is barraging him with questions. Cruise demands Nicholson's character tell him the truth, and the response comes as an outburst, "You can't handle the truth!" In another example, we know that a six-year old doesn't have the capacity to hear or understand something meant for someone forty years older.

Prophetic people can have the tendency to think that they should always know what God is doing in someone else's life and even in their own, but such is often not the case.

Yes, God will keep stuff from us…

You Can't Have What Belongs to You

We may ask why some people seem to have a greater measure of the anointing than others, and while there can be a number of reasons, I'll offer you two.

It is God Himself who determines who gets which gifts and the capacity of each person to carry them. We read this in 1 Corinthians chapter 12:

"But the manifestation of the Spirit is given to each one for the profit of all: for to one is given the word of wisdom through the Spirit, to another the word of knowledge through the same Spirit, to another faith by the same Spirit, to another gifts of healings by [a]the same Spirit, to another the working of miracles, to another prophecy, to another discerning of spirits, to another different kinds of tongues, to another the interpretation of tongues. But one and the same Spirit works all these things, distributing to each one individually as He wills." (12: 7-11 NKJV)

Romans 12:3-4: "For I say, through the grace given to me, to everyone who is among you, not to think of himself more highly than he ought to think, but to think soberly, as God has dealt to each one a measure of faith. For as we have many members in one body, but all the members do not have the same function."

And then we have the reason associated with the title of this topic - we can't have what belongs to us. Why, you might wonder?

The answer is summarized in Luke 16 in the parable of the unjust steward, a man who is improperly managing money that doesn't belong to him. (God, who owns everything, has given us the same responsibility to steward, or manage money which doesn't belong to us.) At parable's end we see the consequence of being unfaithful with something that belongs to someone else.

Luke 16:10-12 (NKJV): "He who is faithful in what is least is faithful also in much; and he who is unjust in what is least is unjust also in much. Therefore if you have not been faithful in the unrighteous mammon, who will commit to your trust the true riches? And if you have not been faithful in what is another man's, who will give you what is your own?"

The principle here is that if we've been unfaithful in what belongs to God then God can't release to us what's ours.

So when I hear people question their anointing or the level of it, one of the things that comes to mind is whether that person is being faithful in their giving.

If we're unfaithful in what belongs to another (God), then we shouldn't expect God to release to us what He intended, or even expect something bigger.

Lessons from Ziklag

I want you to put yourself in David's shoes and really contemplate the depth of his emotion and that of his men as they return from fighting the Philistines:

1 Samuel 30:1-6 (NKJV): "Now it happened, when David and his men came to Ziklag, on the third day, that the Amalekites had invaded the South and Ziklag, attacked Ziklag and burned it with fire, and had taken captive the women and those who were there, from small to great; they did not kill anyone, but carried them away and went their way. So David and his men came to the city, and there it was, burned with fire; and their wives, their sons, and their daughters had been taken captive. Then David and the people who were with him lifted up their voices and wept, until they had no more power to weep. And David's two wives, Ahinoam the Jezreelitess, and Abigail the widow of Nabal the Carmelite, had been taken captive. Now David was greatly distressed, for the people spoke of stoning him, because the soul of all the people was grieved, every man for his sons and his daughters. But David strengthened (encouraged) himself in the Lord his God."

Here are some observations, lessons, and reflective questions to take from Ziklag:

While you're fighting and defeating one enemy, another enemy may attack somewhere else in your life. And yes, it can often be an attack against your family and your finances.

It says that David "was greatly distressed." Ask yourself what your own emotions would be in a similar scenario.

How would you react to having everyone against you, blaming you for the mess you're in?

What do you do when you're totally devastated, your family is being attacked by the enemy, much of what you've worked hard for is gone, and everyone is against you?

You must learn to "encourage yourselves." Yes, you MUST LEARN HOW TO ENCOURAGE YOURSELVES, even if what you really want to do is the opposite, to feel sorry for yourself.

Even in your brokenness you must seek the Lord for His direction.

Now what?

1 Samuel 30:7-10 (NKJV): "Then David said to Abiathar the priest, Ahimelech's son, 'Please bring the ephod here to me.' And Abiathar brought the ephod to David. So David inquired of the Lord, saying, 'Shall I pursue this troop? Shall I overtake them?' And He answered him, 'Pursue, for you shall surely overtake them and without fail recover all.' So David went, he and the six hundred men who were with him, and came to the Brook Besor, where those stayed who were left behind. But David pursued, he and four hundred men; for two

hundred stayed behind, who were so weary that they could not cross the Brook Besor."

g. David prays to find out what God wants him to do and then does it.

h. David has to lead even though he's broken.

i. People who you want to count on to help you, sometimes tell you they can't.

Once the battle is over and you win, what do you do?

1 Samuel 30:22-30: " 'Because they did not go with us, we will not give them any of the spoil that we have recovered, except for every man's wife and children, that they may lead them away and depart.' But David said, 'My brethren, you shall not do so with what the Lord has given us, who has preserved us and delivered into our hand the troop that came against us. For who will heed you in this matter? But as his part is who goes down to the battle, so shall his part be who stays by the supplies; they shall share alike.' So it was, from that day forward; he made it a statute and an ordinance for Israel to this day. Now when David came to Ziklag, he sent some of the [d]spoil to the elders of Judah, to his friends, saying, 'Here is a present for you from the spoil of the enemies of the Lord'— to those who were in Bethel, those who were in Ramoth of the South, those who were in Jattir, those who were in Aroer, those who were in Siphmoth, those who were in Eshtemoa, those who were in Rachal, those who were in the cities of the Jerahmeelites, those who were in the cities of the Kenites, those who were in Hormah, those who were in Chorashan, those who were in Athach, those who were in Hebron,

and to all the places where David himself and his men were accustomed to rove."

j. You must remember that although people you were counting on didn't go to this battle, they did go to many others. This realization will go a long way in affirming relationship as opposed to rewarding performance.

k. If at all possible, pass on your blessings to as many people as you can.

l. God will take your deepest tragedies and turn them into triumphs.

Follow Me

I had just taken the dogs out at 5:30 this morning, and as I was standing on our back deck waiting for Hammett, our oldest Dalmatian, I felt like Jesus stepped onto the deck.

It became very quiet and then I heard him say, "Follow Me." I stood there stunned and then immediately realized that I was alone again. Even as I write this, these two words are echoing in my mind - FOLLOW ME...

It wasn't as if He was saying to follow what other people said about Him. There were two very simple words that carry a profound meaning. Can you hear them? FOLLOW ME... They are only two words, yet I can experience their depth. Can you?

When I got in the house I made my way to my computer and typed in "Follow me." As I was reading the various scriptures in the New

Testament, I came across Matthew 16:21-25 in The Contemporary English Version.

Before I comment (which is probably unnecessary), I can feel/sense Jesus looking over my shoulder watching what I am writing. He bends down and whispers in my ear, "Brian, you need to follow me. What I have planned for you and how you must follow me is different from how I will have others follow me."

He reminds me that there is a price to be paid, a cost which many of His children have been unwilling to pay. He says that their eyes are focused only on the cost itself and not the joy beyond it. Many scriptures are flooding my mind. One is the story of the rich young ruler who won't give up everything to follow Jesus. Though he refuses to follow Jesus, the scripture says that Jesus loved him. (Mark 10:21) Praise God that when we don't follow him fully, He still loves us.

Perhaps we need a Selah moment, a time to pause and mediate…

Let's read Matthew 16:21-25 (CEV): "From then on, Jesus began telling his disciples what would happen to him. He said, 'I must go to Jerusalem. There the nation's leaders, the chief priests, and the teachers of the Law of Moses will make me suffer terribly. I will be killed, but three days later I will rise to life.' Peter took Jesus aside and told him to stop talking like that. He said, 'God would never let this happen to you, Lord!' Jesus turned to Peter and said, 'Satan, get away from me! You're in my way because you think like everyone else and not like God.' Then Jesus said to his disciples: 'If any of you want to be my followers, you must forget about yourself. You must take up your cross and follow me. If you want to save your life, you will destroy it. But if you give up your life for me, you will find it.' "

I started writing what I saw in these six verses and then was told not to. I would love to hear what you see in them. What is Jesus whispering in your ear?

Can you hear it? FOLLOW ME, YOU FOLLOW ME. We must avoid what Peter said in John 21:20-21: "Then Peter, turning around, saw the disciple whom Jesus loved following, who also had leaned on His breast at the supper, and said, 'Lord, who is the one who betrays You?' Peter, seeing him, said to Jesus, 'But Lord, what about this man?'"

Here is Jesus' response to Peter, "Jesus said to him, 'If I will that he remain till I come, what is that to you? You follow Me.'" (verse 22)

Don't be concerned about others - YOU FOLLOW ME...

Ready or Not, Here I Come

As a little boy I played Hide and Seek, a game children still enjoy today. One child closes his eyes, counts to ten, and then opens them, announcing loudly, "Ready or not, here I come!" Then this child who is "it" searches for the other children who have hidden in various places.

If you listen carefully you will hear the same announcement, "Ready or not, here I come." It's the voice of God telling all of us that He's coming regardless of whether or not we're ready to receive Him.

If you're one who's hiding; it's silly because there's no place that you can go where He doesn't see you. If you're running, don't look now, but He's right beside you. Can you see the smile on His face? Those who are overwhelmed by hopelessness and despair can open their eyes to discover that He's right there with you. You see, whether or not YOU'RE ready, Abba is seeking you out...

Jeremiah 23:24 (New English Translation): " 'Do you really think anyone can hide himself where I cannot see him?' the Lord asks. 'Do you not know that I am everywhere?' the Lord asks."

Remember Adam and Eve in Genesis chapter three when they get tired of hiding from God? They didn't know that there was no place where His love and mercy couldn't find them. He's relentless in His pursuit of us...

I am convinced our Father has made up his mind, and we're going to see the evidence:

Joel 2:28-29: "And it shall come to pass afterward That I will pour out My Spirit on all flesh; Your sons and your daughters shall prophesy, Your old men shall dream dreams, Your young men shall see visions. And also on My menservants and on My maidservants I will pour out My Spirit in those days."

It's not about us being ready. It's about Him keeping His promise to mankind.

There is a voice covering the earth like an early morning fog or mist. He is pursuing us, bringing us to the very place we want to be. This is also where He wants us to be. We were created for this place. He is gathering an army to impact the world with the presence that each of you carry, His presence.

2 Corinthians 2:15 (NKJV): "For we are to God the fragrance of Christ among those who are being saved and among those who are perishing."

The funny thing is that even if we think we're ready, we really aren't, because what He's going to do we wouldn't be able to comprehend even if He told us.

Habakkuk 1:5 (NKJV): "Look among the nations and watch— Be utterly astounded! For I will work a work in your days Which you would not believe, though it were told you."

READY OR NOT, HERE I COME... We are going to be ASTOUNDED!

Set Things in Order, the Things That Are Lacking

For years now I've been hearing the Holy Spirit tell me to do all that I can to be ready for what God wants to do. I realize that as much as I prepare, I'm still going to be astonished. Even though I won't be fully ready, I still need to do all that I can to learn, grow, and change, and to allow my character to be shaped more into His likeness.

With those thoughts in mind, we'll see that Titus was left behind on the island of Crete to prepare the church and its leadership to be all that God intended.

I promise you that there will be times when you'll be left behind too. You might feel slighted, but cherish these moments. God is preparing you. He is having us set things in order in our lives so that we'll be the "church" he wants each of us to be.

Titus 1:5 (NKJV): "For this reason I left you in Crete, that you should set in order the things that are lacking, and appoint elders in every city as I commanded you."

It's a time and a season to get ready:

Revelation 19:7 (NKJV): "Let us be glad and rejoice and give Him glory, for the marriage of the Lamb has come, and His wife has made herself ready."

This point is really driven home in the life of Esther when she is one of the "contestants" among the virgins preparing to be chosen queen.

Esther 2:12 (NKJV): "Each young woman's turn came to go in to King Ahasuerus after she had completed twelve months' preparation, according to the regulations for the women, for thus were the days of their preparation apportioned: six months with oil of myrrh, and six months with perfumes and preparations for beautifying women."

Verses 16-17: "So Esther was taken to King Ahasuerus, into his royal palace, in the tenth month, which is the month of Tebeth, in the seventh year of his reign. The king loved Esther more than all the other women, and she obtained grace and favor in his sight more than all the virgins; so he set the royal crown upon her head and made her queen instead of Vashti."

Yes, you read it: one entire year preparing. Our own preparation time is usually much longer... The point is that we're all being prepared to be used by God.

2 Timothy 2:20-22 (TPT): "In a palace you find many kinds of containers and tableware for many different uses. Some are beautifully inlaid with gold or silver, but some are made of wood or earthenware; some of them are used for banquets and special occasions, and some for everyday use. But you, Timothy, must not see your life and ministry this way. Your life and ministry must not be disgraced, for you are to be a

pure container of Christ and dedicated to the honorable purposes of your Master, prepared for every good work that he gives you to do."

Redeem the time you have and get ready to be used by God.

The Revelation Approach

Looking back at the period when I was counseling people and needing to confront them about various matters, I recognize my failure at approaching them in the right way. Rarely did I speak to them in a manner where they could hear what I needed to say.

Let's look at how the Holy Spirit approached the church of Ephesus. First, he encourages them, tells them what they're doing right, and commends them. Next, he points out where they need to change (repent) and then tells them of the blessing and reward they'll receive if they do.

If we're approached in this manner we're typically more willing to listen. Thankfully after learning the hard way, I have used this approach for many, many years since and can say it works.

Here is Revelation 2:1-7: "To the [a]angel of the church of Ephesus write, 'These things says He who holds the seven stars in His right hand, who walks in the midst of the seven golden lampstands: 'I know your works, your labor, your [b]patience, and that you cannot [c]bear those who are evil. And you have tested those who say they are apostles and are not, and have found them liars; and you have persevered and have patience, and have labored for My name's sake and have not become weary. Nevertheless I have this against you, that you have left your first love. Remember therefore from where you have fallen; repent and do the first works, or else I will come to you quickly and remove your lampstand from its place—unless you repent. But this you have, that you hate the deeds of the Nicolaitans, which I also hate. He who has an ear, let him hear what the Spirit says to the churches. To him who overcomes I will give to eat from the tree of life, which is in the midst of the Paradise of God.' "

Try this approach with people. You'll find it disarms them and creates an atmosphere and willingness to hear.

Soul Ties

What are soul ties? Are they good or bad?

Soul ties occur when two hearts are united together, a thing which can be either positive or negative. An example of a positive soul tie is when two people get married and become one flesh: "For this reason a man shall leave his father and mother and be joined to his wife, and the two shall become one flesh." (Matthew 19:5, NKJV)

Then there are unhealthy soul ties:

1 Corinthians 6:16 (NKJV): "Or do you not know that he who is joined to a harlot is one body with her?" For "the two," he says, "shall become one flesh."

We see examples of people becoming attached to one another and it leading to unbiblical consequences:

Genesis 34:1-3 (NKJV): "Now Dinah the daughter of Leah, whom she had borne to Jacob, went out to see the daughters of the land. And when Shechem the son of Hamor the Hivite, prince of the country, saw her, he took her and lay with her, and violated her. His soul was strongly attracted to Dinah the daughter of Jacob, and he loved the young woman and spoke kindly to the young woman."

Genesis 34:8(NKJV): "But Hamor spoke with them, saying, 'The soul of my son Shechem longs for your daughter. Please give her to him as a wife.'"

Unhealthy soul ties result in another person having a part of us. This usually occurs through sexual intimacy. It can also happen when two people form a deep bond through words they speak to one another. The result is that one or both parties are consumed with the other, always wondering where the other is and what they're doing. Even though they may not want them on their mind, they are. They may also want to be with the other person even though they know it's not a good thing.

So what do we do when someone has a part of us that they shouldn't? Let's look at their connection to us as a spiritual umbilical-cord. When a child is born he or she is attached to the mother until the umbilical cord is cut. When we are attached to someone we shouldn't be, we likewise need to cut, or sever our attachment.

Wherever there's been an unhealthy or unbiblical soul tie, that person still has a part of another until that person takes it back. This needs to happen when a person has had a soul tie with someone other than their husband or wife, because otherwise it can be difficult to give their whole self to their mate when someone else has part of them. Soul ties can therefore be a terrible weapon of the enemy.

Thankfully soul ties can be easily broken through prayer when we renounce our past attachments and then take back what was given away. God restores and redeems everything.

The principle is seen in 2 Corinthians 4:2:

"But we have renounced the hidden things of shame," renounce meaning "to cut or sever." (NKJV)

There are healthy soul ties as with David and Jonathan. Their relationship really demonstrates what true friendship can be like. It's worth the time to examine:

1 Samuel 18:1-3: "As soon as he had finished speaking to Saul, the soul of Jonathan was knit to the soul of David, and Jonathan loved him as his own soul. And Saul took him that day and would not let him return to his father's house. Then Jonathan made a covenant with David, because he loved him as his own soul."

If you have memories of past relationships, wanting to revisit them or at least fantasize about them; if you desire someone other than your mate or are consumed with thinking about someone, you might want to consider breaking your attachment and being set free.

Jesus, Help Them to Know

I've written this book to offer you some gems that I've found in Our Father's River.

I can't begin to recount how many times when I think of you that my eyes fill with tears and my heart begins to ache. Even many times during the writing of this book, tears would fill my eyes.

I groan and cry out in my Spirit. My desire for all of you with everything in me is that you would KNOW WHO YOU ARE, THAT YOU WOULD KNOW HOW MUCH THE FATHER LOVES YOU, that YOU ARE SPECIAL AND ANOINTED, AND that GOD HAS BIG PLANS FOR YOU. THIS IS YOUR HOUR, YOUR TIME - DON'T HOLD BACK...

I can so identify with Paul as he writes in Second Corinthians and also in Galatians:

"I wrote to you in floods of tears, out of great trouble and anguish in my heart, not so that I could make you sad but so that you would know just how much overflowing love I have towards you." (2 Cor. 2:3 NTE)

"My little children, for whom I am again in [the pains of] labor until Christ is [completely and permanently] formed within you." (Gal. 4: 18-20 AMP)

I'll end with this passage in First Thessalonians:

"For what is our hope, or joy, or crown of rejoicing? Is it not even you in the presence of our Lord Jesus Christ at His coming?" (2:19, NKJV)

ABOUT THE AUTHOR

Pastor Brian R. Weeks began ministering in 1972 and has served as a pastor to both youth and young adults. He also served as an associate pastor for eleven years, and then for 25 years as a senior pastor, apostolic missionary, and church planter. In March of 2017 he released his church Solomon's Porch, but in order to remain part of the local church, continues to serve among its several pastors.

In 2008 Pastor Brian formed Brian Weeks Ministries to facilitate his call to travel nationally and internationally. His travels have taken him to Haiti, Ukraine, India, Romania, the Dominican Republic, Canada, and Moldova. He has ministered in evangelical, charismatic, Episcopal, Catholic, black pentecostal, Dutch Reform, Vineyard, Methodist, Baptist, Anglican, and Faith Churches.

His ministry includes teaching, training leaders and pastors through pastors' conferences, youth conferences, and Bible Schools, as well as doing prophetic ministry in these same settings.

Pastor Brian has co-planted two churches and has planted three others. His most recent church plant was birthed on Christmas Eve 2009. With his rich and diversified experience, he loves encouraging and mentoring other pastors in the Holy Spirit, as well as helping them grow and develop their churches into their respective futures.

Pastor Brian's passion is to see lives transformed by the power and love of God. His strong desire is that God's sons and daughters would not only discover their gifts and talents, but more importantly, comprehend how much God delights in them and how affectionately they are loved, knowing full well that they were created for a divine purpose. Pastor Brian's prophetic ministry helps people grasp these realities and empowers them to take steps towards their tomorrows. One of his greatest joys is to see people delight in God's presence and cherish their relationship with the Lord and with His people.

Pastor Brian lives in Rehoboth, Massachusetts with his wife Donna of forty-six years. They have two adult children.

Made in the USA
Middletown, DE
05 March 2023